Northwest Foraging

by Doug Benoliel

illustrated by Mark Orsen

A guide to edible plants of the Pacific Northwest

Cover Design by Tom McMacken

Acknowledgement

My curiosity and excitement about plants began when at the age of 6 or 7 I successfully transplanted a lettuce plant that I was told wouldn't grow. To both my Father and Mother I express appreciation for letting me play-work in the vegie and flower gardens. Many sunny hours were spent and summer money earned while working with plants in the years that followed.

Formal education started at the University of Washington, where I enjoyed many good botany instructors, including Clarence Muhlick, C. Leo Hitchcock, Daniel Stuntz, and Weston Blaser. Dr. Blaser has been of much direct assistance in the last 6 months in reading and correcting the manuscript and making valuable suggestions. Thanks.

Following graduation the opportunity to learn and teach at the National Outdoor Leadership School in Lander, Wyoming, for 3 summers added much to my first-hand experiences of living with and eating mountain plants. Those experiences and people will stay with me for a long time.

Thanks goes to the people who directly and indirectly helped to put together the unique recipe section. Special appreciation goes to Tamara Buchanan for her friendship and imagination.

There have been other persons who have encouraged me in the progress of the manuscript, some of whom are Nels and Bren, Ron and Gail, Johanna, the people at Signpost, and the Group. I further wish to thank all the people who have been a part of the edible plant classes that I have taught in the last 2 years. I would look forward to each class, not knowing what new information I would learn about people or plants.

I have tried to make this book an expression of first-hand experiences. However, it was necessary at times to refer to the literature on the subject. I wish to acknowledge some of the fine books that were extremely useful. They are: **Vascular Plants of the Pacific Northwest** (University of Washington Press) by C. Leo Hitchcock, Arthur Cronquist, Marion Ownbey, and J. W. Thompson for super fine descriptions; **Wildflowers of the Pacific Coast** (Binfords & Mort) by Leslie Haskins; **Ethnobotany of Western Washington** (University of Washington Press) by Erna Gunther for accountings of Indian usage of plants; **A Field Guide to Rocky Mountain Wildflowers** (Houghton Mifflin Company) by John and Frank Craighead, and Ray Davis for interesting notes about plants; and **Poison Plants of the United States and Canada** (Prentice-Hall Inc.) by John Kingsbury. Other books were also of help. Most of these appear in the "Suggested Further Reading" section at the end of the book.

Foreword

Popular interest in "natural" foods and medicinal and kitchen herbs has had a great surge in recent years. Unfortunately, some books and frequent statements in advertising and the press are either misleading or dishonest. Folk science is often more interesting than true. Since science seems rigid and cold, we often find greater comfort in the familiar, the "homey" - and at times in "magic".

In this volume, Doug Benoliel has selected from an enormous amount of popular literature. He presents a careful guide to locally significant nature plants. He warns against the major dangers (or common human frailties) and suggests only foods that he has used and can recommend. His methods have been tested by students in his classes.

There are a large number of teas that have special interest to me. Some of the claims of the curative power of tea are highly exaggerated in some of our literature. To me, the most important value of tea (any kind) is the chance to sit down, wait for the tea to cool enough to drink, and to chat with friends. It isn't medicine or magic - it's calmness in a busy world.

Seeing plants in the field, whether you collect them or not, and making a start in your own plant exploration can be rewarding. This manual can help in many ways.

June 11, 1974   H. Weston Blaser

Other Signpost Publications

High Trails: Guide to the Pacific Crest Trail in Washington
Kayak & Canoe Trips in Washington
Water Trails of Washington
Boulders & Cliffs
Backpacking With Babies
The Packrat Papers

Contents

How To Use This Book

This book is intended to be used as a field guide for the identification of some specific edible and poisonous plants of the Pacific Northwest. The edible ones that are described are ones that, to one degree or another, fall into the categories of being easy to identify, excellent eating, of special interest to the hiker-camper, of special interest to the person living in the city, or a combination of the above. Other edible plants occur in these areas, however, I have included only those that I can recommend. There are many "survival or emergency foods" of questionable value that are not discussed in this book. The poisonous plants described are either highly toxic, common place, or likely to be confused with some edible plant.

I have tried to describe the plants as simply as possible yet accurately enough so that any particular plant could not be confused for a similar one. To accomplish this, some technical words are used, and their meanings can be found in the glossary at the end of the book.

The diversity of the plants described in this book precludes any convenient grouping, so the plants are listed in alphabetical order according to their common names.

In most instances each plant is described in terms of the following: Form, Leaves, Flower, Fruit, Habitat, and Edibility (Poisonous for those of this character). These divisions are particularly useful in field recognition.

With the description of the plants there appears a translation of the Latin names. The Latin or botanical name is comprised of a genus and a species. The genus is the first word and often tells something about the plant's natural history. For example, the generic name, **Rosa**, is the classical Latin name for the Rose. **Pteridium**, the genus of Bracken Fern, comes from the Latin word 'pteron', meaning wing, referring to the leaves representing wings. This is an expression of an early botanist's imagination of the fern attempting to escape from the ground. **Saxifraga** comes from the Latin words 'saxum', rock, and 'grangere', to break, referring to the use of this plant by herbalists in the treatment of "stones" of the urinary tract.

The species name is generally an adjective that describes some feature of the plant. **Laciniatus** means torn and refers to the many divisions of each leaflet in **Rubus laciniatus**, the Evergreen Blackberry. **Maculatum** means spotted, in reference to the purple spots on the stems of **Conium maculatum**, Poison Hemlock. This particular feature of Poison Hemlock is one of the primary means of identification. Another illustration is **angustifolium**, which means narrow-leaf and aptly describes the foliage of Fireweed, **Epilobium angustifolium**. It is my hope that people using this book will become accustomed to the 'foreign' words and understand that through their use more can be appreciated about the plant.

Botanical names have a further use, for there is only one for any one kind of plant. This helps immensely when trying to cross reference from one book to another or even in conversation with another person. It is not as easy to be exact when using common names. **Chenopodium album**, called Goosefoot, Lamb's Quarter, or Pigweed is often mistaken for **Amaranthus retroflexus**, called Green Amaranth, Redroot, Wild Beet, or Pigweed. Here is a case where a common name, Pigweed, refers to two very different plants. A further point to note is that local differences in common names are frequent.

Common names sometimes describe a feature of the plant. Brook Saxifrage thrives near streams, creeks, and brooks. The fruit of Chokecherry is very bitter, especially the immature fruit, which is toxic. Mountain Sorrel grows only in subalpine and alpine regions. Fireweed grows in areas that have been burned. Both the edible and refreshing Water Cress and the violently poisonous Water Hemlock grow in or near water.

Regrettably, only a few Indian names have been retained. Salal, Camas, and Death Camas are examples. These are plants that were extremely important to the natives of the Pacific Northwest.

An explanation about sprouting, flowering and fruiting as they relate to elevations is important. Primarily because of the lower temperatures and the greater accumulation of snow, spring comes to the high altitudes later than the lowlands. This means that young shoots of such plants as Stinging Nettle, Bracken Fern, and Fireweed can be harvested during May and June at 3,500 feet. It was 2-3 months earlier that these same plants were available for gathering in the fields, meadows, and forests at sea-level.

The drawings for Northwest Foraging have been meticulously prepared, artist and author working together to insure that all details are correct.

Each drawing depicts the plant as it appears in the season when it is best for harvesting. The most important features for identification are emphasized. For example, Shepherd's Purse is shown with the characteristically triangular seed capsule and the uniquely shaped leaves.

All drawings are in proportion to living plants. The scale of the drawings, and the season in which the plant appears as it does in the drawing, is listed at the end of each description. "½x" means that the drawing is one half the actual size of the plant, "1x" means the drawing and the plant are the same size. □

About This Hobby

I find that there is no short-cut to learning and knowing wild edible plants. Rules of thumb are general; they do not always apply. Some of the poisonous plants that occur in the Pacific Northwest are so toxic that making a single mistake in identification may be a person's last. A practical and sound method of teaching oneself plant identification is to learn a few at a time, continually adding to your knowledge with experience.

Use this book as a guide, not the absolute truth. What is written here is an expression of my experiences. Your experiences may differ considerably. For instance, it is important to recognize that each person's body chemistry is different. A plant which one person may be able to eat freely may not settle well with another. Remember, when eating a wild plant for the first time, eat only a small portion to find out how your body responds to the new food.

One of the easiest ways to pick up knowledge is to learn from a person who has expertise in identifying and eating plants. The theme from the previous paragraph is repeated here: regard any teachings as a guide line from which to start.

The taste of wild food is different from those to which most of us are accustomed. Rarely will a "wild green" taste like the greens that can be bought in a supermarket. Also, none of the "imperfections" have been bred out of wild food. The accepted uniformity of taste and texture found in domesticated fruits and vegetables is absent in Mother Nature.

Speaking of supermarkets, if you are expecting to go into the local field or forest and find a shopping cart full of wild goodies, then you most likely will be disappointed. Competing with their neighbors for the available sunlight, soil, and moisture, wild plants do not bear fruit nor grow foliage on the scale of their pampered domestic cousins. It is unusual (without hard work) to find wild salad material that rewards one with as much greenery as a small head of lettuce, or to find a tuberous plant that gives one as much starch as a medium sized potato (the cattail is an exception).

And what, you may ask, are a number of poisonous plants doing in an edible plant book? The poisonous plant section in Northwest Foraging is devoted to plants that could be mistaken for edible ones, very common plants that it would be wise to look out for, or extremely poisonous plants that won't allow more than one mistake in identification. An example is Death Camas, easily mistaken for the edible Camas and the Wild Onion. All three plants have similar physical characteristics and grow in similar habitats. Another poisonous plant one needs to be aware of is Poison Hemlock, often mistaken for Wild Carrot. Both are members of the Parsley family and have similar foliage, growth habits, and root systems. It is so difficult for the novice to tell the two apart that Wild Carrot has not been included in this book. The error in identification of this plant could very well be a fatal one as there is no known antidote for the extremely toxic Poison Hemlock. This is the same plant that was given to the Greek philosopher Socrates. He died within minutes of drinking a tea brewed with the leaves of Poison Hemlock. ☐

Harvesting

The harvesting of wild plants requires care and a bit of foresight. Carefully stripping a few leaves off a number of Fireweed plants instead of pulling up the entire stalk may seem silly in a giant field of this prolific plant, but careless harvesting does take a toll.

Most of the plants described in this book can be found in the lowland rural areas of the Pacific Northwest. Normal precautions while harvesting are adequate here, the precautions coming mostly under the heading of common sense. When only a portion of the plant (leaves, flower, or fruit) is to be used, take only a few from any one plant, and spread your harvesting over as wide an area as possible. Try not to take all of any one thing from any one area. The same principle applies when the entire plant is used, or a part of the plant that when used precludes the survival of that plant (the rhizomes of the cattail for example). Take care, don't ruffle the scenery too much, and both you and the plants will be happy.

Backpackers making use of this book while in the wilderness have a special obligation to the land and the plants. I don't recommend harvesting in or near campsites or along popular trails. Clearcuts often have much edible foliage which can be harvested with minimum danger of disrupting the scenery. Plants can also be found alongside logging roads while driving to or from your wilderness destination. Please note: It is illegal to pick (harvest) any plant material while in a National Park.

One last note on harvesting. Often you will find choice edibles alongside roads. It is illegal to stop on a limited access road for anything other than an emergency. Another consideration: The Highway Departments of most states periodically spray the sides of roads with defoliants, to inhibit plant growth that might cause visibility problems for drivers. Although in the amounts used and considering how much of the foliage you will consume these chemicals are not toxic, knowledge of alien chemicals will be appreciated by many people. ☐

Drying & Storing

The drying process can be a rather simple one, using the available material, space, and equipment that one has on hand. Drying is generally done to preserve the plant matter for later use. Here are 3 examples of drying of different plant parts.

Rose Hips gathered from the field need to be dried within a week or 2 or mold may start to grow. The fruit can be washed and the debris of leaves and stems separated from the orange-red hips. (I use worm-free fruit for jams, jellies, and sauces; it seems that hips from east of the Cascades have fewer worms.) Spread them one layer deep on a flat surface. A cookie sheet works well. Screens let more air circulate and for this reason they work more quickly. Place the container in a warm, ventilated location and in a few weeks, depending on the size of the hips, the fruit will be dry. Check them periodically. Another way is to place the container in an oven set at 100 degrees, and in 2-24 hours the fruit will be dry. This is a very pleasant procedure, for the aroma of drying Rose Hips is sweet. Take care not to toast them; it changes the flavor.

Berries, such as Blue Elderberries, can be dried and stored for later use. Much the same process as mentioned above can be employed. Unlike the Rose Hips, the Blue Elderberries will shrink to ½ their original size. After the moisture is out of the berries, they are ready for storage. The fruit of Salal, Blackberry, Chokecherry, Oregon Grape, and Juneberry can be dried this way.

The drying of fresh greens, often for use in a hot beverage, is rapid if the foliage is placed one layer deep and the container is set in a room with mild air circulation. Sun drying may reduce flavor and according to some people it adversely affects the medicinal value of the plant material. Shrinkage is considerable, so gather lots of leaves. If one is willing to turn the piles every day or 2 to promote uniform drying and to prevent spoilage, greens can be stacked to dry. Sheep Sorrel, Stinging Nettle, Fireweed, Strawberry, and Chickweed are examples of plants for which one uses the foliage for teas.

Storing is easily done by putting the completely dried plant parts in clean dry containers. I prefer mayonnaise jars that have the cardboard inner lid removed. This cardboard can trap moisture. Another favorite is Mickeys Wide Mouth malt liquor jars with corks. Sometimes I think the fun part is collecting these colorful, green jars. They are decorative and inexpensive (if you like malt liquor). The corks are available at most wine supply shops. Place filled containers in a cool dark place. Storing in a sunny window causes the plant material to fade in flavor.

I store rose hips whole and grind them in a coffee mill before use. Berries are stored whole to be reconstituted later with water or syrup. The foliage of plants such as Fireweed, Chickweed, Blackberry, Sheep Sorrel, and Stinging Nettle I store crushed, while preserving the entire leaf of Mint, Kinnikinnick, and Strawberry. I enjoy the whole leaf floating in my tea. □

Seasonal Availability

These are categories indicating which plants are available during each season. The divisions within each category are based upon plant parts, with the further addition that the "greens" are either salad or cooked type. All the salad greens can be used as cooked greens but not vice versa. An example is Stinging Nettle, which is a cooked green but should not be used as a salad green.

SPRING

Salad Greens

Cattail (inner lvs.)
Chickweed
Dandelion
Miner's Lettuce
Oregon Grape (new lvs.)
Wild Onion
Plantain
Lamb's Quarters
Water Cress
Shepherd's Purse
Violet
Siberian Miner's Lettuce
Wood Sorrel
Sheep Sorrel
Winter Cress
Sedum
Thistle (stalk)

Cooked Greens

Asparagus
Bracken Fern
Curly Dock
Mustard
Stinging Nettle
Wild Strawberry (bev.)
Wild Mint (bev.)
Kinnikinnick (bev.)
Fireweed
Thistle (stalk)

Roots

Camas
Cattail
Chocolate Lily
Dandelion (bev.)
Yellow Bell
Wild Onion
Springbeauty
Thistle
Harvest Lily

Berries

Highbush Cranberry
Kinnikinnick

Seed Capsules

Shepherd's Purse
Mustard

Flowers

Mustard
Wild Onion
Shepherd's Purse
Winter Cress
Oregon Grape
Rose
Violet

SUMMER

Salad Greens

Siberian Miner's Lettuce
Miner's Lettuce
Cattail (inner lvs.)
Chickweed
Violet
Sedum (mts.)
Shooting Star (mts.)
Springbeauty (mts.)
Purslane
Brook Saxifrage (mts.)
Dandelion
Avalanche Lily (mts.)
Glacier Lily (mts.)
Mountain Sorrel (mts.)
Water Cress
Wild Onion (mts.)
Shepherd's Purse
Wood Sorrel
Sheep Sorrel
Winter Cress
Lamb's Quarters
Green Amaranth

Cooked Greens

Stinging Nettle
Kinnikinnick (bev.)
Mint (bev.)
Plantain
Curly Dock
Wild Strawberry (bev.)
Thistle (stalk)
Bracken Fern (mts.)

Roots

Burdock
Cattail
Thistle
Wild Onion
Dandelion (bev.)
American Bistort (mts.)
Camas

Glacier Lily (mts.)
Avalanche Lily (mts.)
Chocolate Lily
Yellow Bell
Evening Primrose

Berries

Currants
Thimbleberry
Salmonberry
Pacific Blackberry
Evergreen Blackberry
Himalayan Blackberry
Wild Strawberry
Juneberry
Indian Plum
Oregon Grape
Salal

Seed Capsules

Mustard
Shepherd's Purse
Water Cress

Flowers

Cattail
Pineapple Weed (bev.)
Rose
Glacier Lily (mts.)
Springbeauty (mts.)
Violet (mts.)
Water Cress
Winter Cress
Lamb's Quarters

FALL

Salad Greens

Siberian Miner's Lettuce
Miner's Lettuce
Chickweed
Violet
Water Cress
Wood Sorrel
Sheep Sorrel
Purslane

Cooked Greens

Fireweed
Wild Strawberry
Kinnikinnick (bev.)
Blackberry (bev.)
Shooting Star (mts.)
Sedum (mts.)

Roots

Cattail
Wild Onion
Dandelion

Berries

Chokecherry
Blue Elderberry
Kinnikinnick
Huckleberry
Blueberry
Juneberry (mts.)
Salal
Oregon Grape
Evergreen Blackberry
Thimbleberry (mts.)

Seeds

Rose (hips)
Lamb's Quarters
Purslane
Shepherd's Purse
Hazelnut
Green Amaranth

WINTER

Salad Greens

Siberian Miner's Lettuce
Chickweed
Violet
Sheep Sorrel
Water Cress
Winter Cress
Wood Sorrel

Cooked Greens

Strawberry (bev.)

Roots

Cattail
Wild Onion

Berries

Highbush Cranberry
Kinnikinnick

Seeds

Curly Dock
Lamb's Quarters
Rose (hips)

Seasons For Beverage Plants

Blackberry	leaves	Sp S F W
Blue Elderberry	flowers	Sp S
Chickweed	leaves & stems	Sp S F W
Dandelion	leaves & roots	Sp S F W
Fireweed	leaves	Sp S F
Kinnikinnick	leaves	Sp S F W
Mint	leaves	Sp S F
Mountain Sorrel	leaves	S
Nettle	leaves	Sp S F
Pineapple Weed	flowers	Sp S F
Sheep Sorrel	leaves	Sp S F W
Strawberry	leaves	Sp S F W
Salmonberry	leaves	Sp S F
Thimbleberry	leaves	Sp S F
Rose	fruit (hip)	F W
Wood Sorrel	leaves	Sp S
Yarrow	leaves, flowers, seeds	Sp S F

Plant Habitats

East of Cascades

Asparagus
Bittersweet Nightshade (P)
Blue Elderberry
Buttercup (P)
Cattail
Chickweed
Camas
Chokecherry
Dandelion
Shooting Star
Curly Dock
Miner's Lettuce
Death Camas (P)
Rose
Juneberry
Gold Currant
Squaw Currant
Mustard
Wild Mint
Plantain
Purslane
Larkspur (P)
Lupine (P)
Church Bell
Chocolate Lily
Avalanche Lily
Glacier Lily
Harvest Lily
Shepherd's Purse
Sheep Sorrel
Springbeauty
Lamb's Quarters
Water Hemlock (P)
Poison Hemlock (P)
Wild Strawberry
Thistle
Wild Onion
Wild Rose
Yarrow
Violet
Water Cress

Fields and Meadows less than 2,000 feet, West of Cascades

Bittersweet Nightshade (P)
Bracken Fern
Buttercup (P)
Curly Dock
Chickweed
Dandelion
Evergreen Blackberry
Evening Primrose
Fireweed
Juneberry
Himalayan Blackberry
Indian Plum
Lupine (P)
Wild Mint
Mustard
Oregon Grape
Poison Hemlock (P)
Pacific Blackberry
Plantain
Red Elderberry (P)
Red Huckleberry
Squashberry
Salmonberry
Siberian Miner's Lettuce
Sheep Sorrel
Stinging Nettle
Wild Strawberry
Thistle
Thimbleberry
Violet
Yarrow
Winter Cress
Wild Cucumber (P)
Wild Rose

Mountains above 2,000 feet

American Bistort
Avalanche Lily
Bog Cranberry
Brook Saxifrage
Bleeding Heart (P)
Buttercup (P)
Blue Elderberry
Sheep Sorrel
Springbeauty
Grouseberry
Dandelion
Fireweed
Foxglove (P)
Juneberry
False Hellebore (P)
Glacier Lily
Golden Currant
Kinnikinnick
Larkspur (P)
Lupine (P)
Mountain Death Camas (P)
Mountain Sorrel
Red Elderberry (P)
Pacific Blackberry
Oval-leaved Blueberry
Salal
Sedum
Sheep Sorrel
Plantain
Shooting Star
Siberian Miner's Lettuce
Stinging Nettle
Springbeauty
Swamp Laurel (P)
Squaw Currant
Violet
Wild Onion
Wild Strawberry
Wild Rose
Wood Sorrel

Conifer Forests west of the Cascades

Baneberry (P)
Bracken Fern

Bleeding Heart (P)
Buttercup (P)
Curly Dock
Dandelion
Fireweed
Foxglove (P)
Hazelnut
Evergreen Blackberry
Himalayan Blackberry
Indian Plum
Juneberry
Kinnikinnick
Miner's Lettuce
Pacific Blackberry
Oregon Grape
Red Huckleberry
Red Elderberry (P)
Salal
Squashberry
Salmonberry
Sheep Sorrel
Siberian Miner's Lettuce
Stinging Nettle
Thimbleberry
Violet
Water Cress
Wood Sorrel
Wild Cucumber

Extremely Wet Habitats

Bittersweet Nightshade (P)
Buttercup (P)
Brook Saxifrage
Bog Cranberry
Cattail
Evergreen Huckleberry
False Hellebore (P)
Plantain
Stinging Nettle
Swamp Laurel (P)
Water Hemlock (P)
Water Cress
Wild Mint

Urban Settings west of the Cascades

Bittersweet Nightshade (P)
Chickweed
Foxglove (P)
Evergreen Blackberry
Dandelion
Lamb's Quarters
Sheep Sorrel
Himalayan Blackberry
Shepherd's Purse
Green Amaranth
Plantain
Purslane
Red Elderberry (P)
Pacific Blackberry
Poison Hemlock (P)
Pineapple Weed

———————————

Introduced Wild Edible Plants

It is interesting to note the number of wild plants in the Pacific Northwest which are not native to this area. Many presently common plants were not found here until quite recently. Listed here are the plants covered in this book which were introduced to this area. "Escaped from Cultivation" means that the agricultural variety of the plant found the accommodations to their liking enough to move in, so to speak.

Asparagus	*
Bittersweet Nightshade	Eurasia
Burdock	Eurasia
Chickweed	Eurasia
Curly Dock	Europe
Dandelion	Europe
English Plantain	Eurasia
Evergreen Blackberry	Europe *
Foxglove	Europe
Himalayan Blackberry	Europe *
Lamb's Quarters	Eurasia
Mint	Europe *
Mustard	Eurasia
Purslane	Europe
Poison Hemlock	Eurasia
Sheep Sorrel	Europe
Shepherd's Purse	Europe
Water Cress	Europe
Winter Cress	Eurasia

*Escaped from culivation

Edible
Plants

American Bistort

American Bistort (Mountain-meadow Knotweed)
Polygonum bistortoides Pursh
Buckwheat Family - Polygonaceae

The edibility of the starchy rootstock of the American Bistort was known to the Blackfoot and the Cheyenne Indians and should be known to the hiker. It is plentiful, easy to identify, and nutritious. Eat only a small quantity until your system is used to the new food. The roots are eaten by rodents and bears, the foliage by elk and deer.

FORM - 1 or more 4-20 inch tall flowering stems; white tufts (flower clusters) atop the stem; jointed stems; primarily basal leaves; shallow rooted, thickened rootstock; inconspicuous plant when not in flower.

LEAVES - mostly basal; lance-shaped or wider; 1-4 inches long; short leaf stalk; stem leaves few and reduced in size.

FLOWER - small white to pinkish in showy clusters, 1-2 inches long, terminal flower cluster; rank scented; June-Sept.

HABITAT - moist soils; full sun; alpine slopes, meadows, streambanks; grows in great numbers, often covering an entire field; 2,000 to 8,000 feet.

EDIBILITY - good. Leaves are good raw in salads, boiled like spinach, and used in soups and stews. The long and enlarged rootstock can be dug and washed. It is eaten raw or cooked. Slice a few and saute them in lots of butter and onions. Serve rice and add soy sauce. The entire rootstock can be peeled and put into soups for a texture addition.

The generic name, *Polygonum*, comes from the Greek words 'poly' meaning many and 'gonu' meaning knee. *Bistortoides* means twice bent. Both names refer to the angularity of the stem, which makes a bend at each node or joint.

drawing: Summer—Fall; ½x

Asparagus

Asparagus
Asparagus officinalis L.
Lily Family - Liliaceae

As yet I have been unable to find Asparagus growing in the wilds west of the Cascades. It thrives in soils that are alkaline and semi-dry, like those in eastern Washington.

FORM - early spring shoots ⅛ to 1 inch in diameter; scaly leaves close to the shoot; developed plant is free branching and 3-5 feet tall; bright red berries in late summer; perennial herb that dies back each year.

HABITAT + the plants in the wild have escaped from cultivation; plentiful in moist areas of eastern Washington and Oregon; fence rows, irrigation ditches, orchards, creek banks; sea-level to 3,000 feet.

EDIBILITY - excellent. Use the young shoots as you would the store bought Asparagus. Regrettably, these tender shoots are available only in April and May. When out harvesting Asparagus, look for the dead, brown stalks of last year. At their bases are the delivious new shoots, which should be cut at ground level.

Asparagus is the ancient Greek name for this plant. *Officinalis* means medicinal.

drawing: Spring; 1x

Blackberry

Blackberries
Pacific Blackberry   *Rubus ursinus* Cham. & Schlecht.
Himalayan Blackberry   *Rubus procerus* Muell.
Evergreen Blackberry   *Rubus laciniatus* Willd.
Rose Family - Rosaceae

The Blackberries need only a little explanation, for they are one of the most common and invasive plants in this region. The Evergreen and the Himalayan Blackberries are found in the city and the rural setting. They grow in vacant lots, along fence rows, open fields; and numerous other niches. The Pacific Blackberry, which is our only native Blackberry, is found in the vacant city lot but more frequently it grows in elevations from 2,000-6,000 feet.

All make excellent eating. The large berries of the Himalayan are the ones most commonly used for pies, preserves, and wine. Fifteen minutes labor can reward one with berries for a couple of pies and a milk shake (to be drunk while making the pies). The small but flavorful fruit of the Pacific Blackberry is considered by many persons to be of top notch quality. This plant was used as parent material to produce several horticultural varieties, including loganberry, youngberry, boysenberry, and others.

The following are basic descriptions of the three Blackberries.

The Pacific Blackberry has slender stems that trail along the ground or over stumps, rocks, or other plants. This is the plant that a woodland traveler trips over as he travels through a logged area. The leaves are composed of 3 leaflets that are toothed. Since the male flowers and female flowers are found on separate plants, one will only find fruit on some of the Pacific Blackberries (the female plants).

The Himalayan Blackberry has large stiff branches that are heavily armed with tough thorns. The branches, 10-30 feet long, command the territory they occupy. 5 thorny, toothed leaflets comprise a single leaf.

The Evergreen Blackberry is much like the Himalayan in general appearance. However, the 5 leaflets are deeply toothed or divided and are rather persistent throughout the year. The Evergreen and Himalayan are escaped from cultivation and occur primarily west of the Cascades. The fruit of both can be harvested from July-August.

Rubus is the ancient Latin name for a member of this genus. *Ursinus* means pertaining to bears and most likely refers to the bristliness of the fruit. *Procerus* means tall and probably refers to the stature of the plant. *Laciniatus* means torn and is used to describe the many divisions of the leaf.

drawing: top to bottom,
Pacific Blackberry— Summer; ½x
Himalayan Blackberry— Summer; ¼x
Evergreen Blackberry8 Late Summer; ¼x

Blue Elderberry

Blue Elderberry
Sambucus cerulea Raf.
Honeysuckly Family - Caprifoliaceae

The Blue Elderberry most commonly grows east of the Cascades, although I have found specimens growing in several locales in western Washington. The Red Elderberry, which is considered in the poisonous section of this book, is the predominant species west of the Cascades. It differs from Blue Elderberry by flowering earlier (April-May), the flower cluster is pyramidal in shape, and the fruit is red.

I have used the dried fruit of the Blue Elderberry in stuffing a cornish game hen. The ingredients are rice, wheat germ, crumbs of a muffin, chopped onion & celery, mung sprouts, raisins, walnuts, dried Blue Elderberry fruit, and an array of spices. When dinner was completed, we had eaten all the stuffing, while half of the bird still remained!

FORM - shrub with several pithy stems; 6-20 feet tall; a single trunk, or several stems.

LEAVES - oppositely arranged on the stem; 5-9 leaflets with each leaflet lance-shaped and 2-5 inches long.

FLOWER - creamy-white; many tiny flowers in a flat-topped cluster being about 10 inches in diameter; erect clusters; June-July.

FRUIT - many pea-sized fruits in a flat-topped cluster; clusters hang down with the weight of the fruit; black or dark blue with a waxy coating; Sept.-Oct.

HABITAT - rich soils; moist locales; open lowlands to nearly timberline; primarily east of the Cascades.

EDIBILITY - excellent. The fruit is used raw or cooked. Use in preserves, pies, hot drinks, or as a substitute for raisins in bird stuffing. The fruit has long been considered to produce an excellent wine. The flowers of this plant are used for Elderflower tea. In the summer when the flower heads are becoming old, put a large paper bag over the flower head and shake. All the ripe petals fall into the sack and one has not destroyed the fertilized flowers, which turn into the fruit of the fall. Consider this a plant to know.

Sambucus is the classical Latin name for a member of this genus. *Cerulea* means blue and refers to the fruit color.

drawing: top to bottom, Summer—Fall; ½x

Blueberry

Blueberry, Huckleberry, Cranberry and Grouseberry
Vaccinium species
Heath Family - Ericaceae

The fruits of these plants are all edible and among the most flavorful of the fruits that one can gather from the wilds. All the plants are so closely related that they are placed in a single genus, *Vaccinium*, from the ancient Latin name for these plants. There are more than a dozen different species in the Pacific Northwest.

All Vacciniums have inconspicuous flowers, which develop into many-seeded berries. They are red, blue, or nearly black in color and with a pleasantly sweet flavor. The leaves are simple, alternately arranged on the stem, and deciduous, except for the Evergreen Huckleberry. Nearly all the stems are angular, some strongly so. A representative sample of the most desired Vacciniums follows.

Red Huckleberry, *V. parvifolium* Smith., is the most abundant *Vaccinium* in the lowland forests west of the Cascades. It is a rather tall shrub, 4-8 feet, with strongly ridged, green stems. The growth characteristic is open and airy, easily employed in the home landscape. It loves rotting wood and shade. The semi-translucent, bright red fruit is ready for harvest in August and September.

The Evergreen Huckleberry, *V. ovatum* Pursh., is the coastal member. This is the only *Vaccinium* that has leaves which last through the winter. The 1 inch long leaves are further featured by saw-toothed margins. The fruit, which is ripe in late summer, is blackish, shiny, and sweet. The berries of some plants turn reddish-brown and lack the juiciness of the black ones. The shrub is highly useful for the ornamental garden. The quality of the foliage, flowers, and fruit is worthy of using in the native garden.

The Oval-leaved Blueberry, *V. ovalifolium* Smith., grows in higher elevations than the Red Huckleberry. The pinkish flowers appear before the oval leaves have reached half their mature size of slightly less than 2 inches. From late August to October one can pick the bluish-black fruit, which is coated with a whitish wax.

The Grouseberry or Whortleberry, *V. scoparium* Leiberg., is the diminutive form of the shrubby Vacciniums. It appears as an irregular green head of a broom protruding from the ground. *Scoparium* means broom. The twiggy stems are completely green. The pale leaves are thin, nearly egg-shaped, and ½ inch long. Being less than 2 feet tall, the plant functions much like a groundcover. Only where one can find a considerable patch of Grouseberry will one be able to harvest any of the semi-translucent red fruit, for the birds and small animals eat them.

The Bog Cranberry, *V. oxycoccos* L., is a creeping, tiny shrub that thrives in bogs and swamps. Sphagnum moss is its companion plant. The small leaves are deep green above and whitish below. The leaf edge is rolled downward. The deep red fruit can reach a size of ½ inch in diameter, looking like an oversized berry on this delicate plant.

drawing: Red Huckleberry, Late Summer; ¾x

Bracken Fern

Bracken Fern (Brake Fern)
Pteridium aquilinum (L.) Kuhn.
Fern Family - Polypodiaceae

There can be much reward in learning this plant, for it can be harvested from April to July, early in the low elevations and later in the mountains. At sea-level the less than 8 inch tall unfolded leaf can be gathered to be used immediately or stored. The season lasts only a few short weeks. However, the plants emerge from the ground later in the season with an increase in altitude. In June and July a person can gather Bracken Fern at 3,000 to 4,500 feet in the Cascades and Olympics. This is a plant that the hiker-camper who wants to supplement his diet should know.

FORM, a perennial that dies back each year, leaving a mass of brown leaves; mature plants 2-4 feet tall; a course fern from a long slender underground root-stock (rhizome); the plant is covered with a reddish-brown "felt".

LEAVES, young leaf curled, looking like a cane and having brown "felt" on it; distinctly 3-forked; 1 leaf arising from the ground; broadly triangular in outline with numerous, oblong to linear divisions; mature spores give brown, velvety appearance to the under-surface in the fall.

HABITAT, full sun to partial shade; well drained soils; generally many plants grow together; extremely abundant plant in the Puget Sound area; fields, burns, moist rich woods, and rock canyons; sea-level to 4,500 feet.

EDIBILITY, excellent *when young*. Cook the young unfolded leaves (fronds) like asparagus. Cook 15 minutes or until tender. The younger they are the more tender and tasteful they will be. Excellent when dipped in a sauce of butter, lemon juice, salt, pepper, chili powder, and onion salt. The fronds can also be boiled, dried, and stored for use later in the year, when they are reconstituted with water.

Pteridium comes from the Latin word 'pteron', meaning wing, referring to the leaves representing wings. This is an expression of an early botanist's imagination of the fern attempting to escape from the ground. *Aquilinum* means eagle-like, referring to the shape and size of the large leaf.

A recent (1973) article in the *American Fern Journal*, Vol. 63, No. 3, titled "Fern Foods of Japan and the Problem of Toxicity" states, "Although the identity of Bracken toxin(s) is yet to be determined it seems clear from contemporary research that the principle involved is both carcinogenic and mutagenic in several kinds of test animals." The article goes on to say that "it appears wise to recommend that the tender, young shoots of Bracken, so widely utilized as an occasional human food, should not be eaten.

The tests described in the article showed that toxicity was reduced by adding salt to the cooking water. This author will continue to eat Bracken Fern, but wishes to point out this new information for the readers own decision.

drawing: Spring; 1x

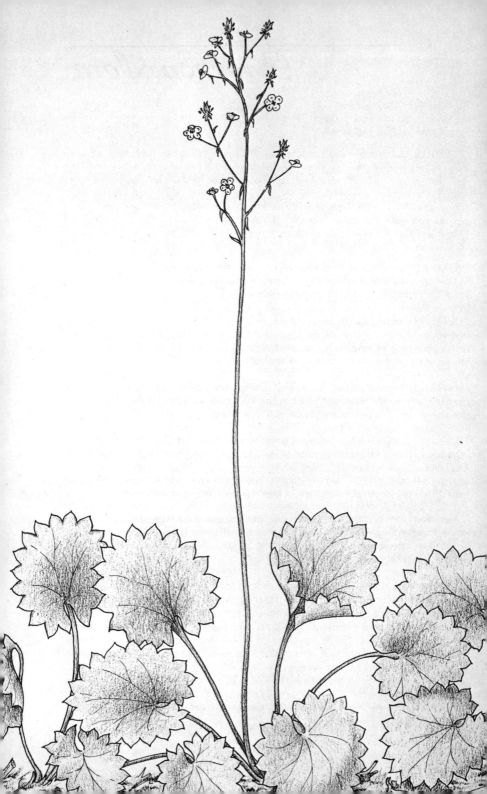

Brook Saxifrage

Brook Saxifrage
Saxifraga arguta D. Don.
Saxifrage Family - Saxifragaceae

I have made many salads from the young tender leaves of Brook Saxifrage. One of the types that I especially enjoy is made from leaves of Brook Saxifrage, Sedum (Stonecrop), Springbeauty, and Mountain Sorrel, with a few reddish flowers of the Mountain Sorrel put on top for color. The salad is ready for eating after spices, vinegar and oil, and chunks of sharp cheddar cheese have been sprinkled over the greens.

FORM - 2-8 inch tall clumps of leaves; low growing perennial; sometimes many plants on a streambank; slender flower stalks in late summer.

LEAVES - basal; numerous; roundish to kidney-shqped; 1-3 inches in diameter; evenly and distinctly toothed; long leaf stalks.

FLOWER - pinkish; inconspicuous; many flowers in a loose cluster; 5-15 inch tall flower stalk; July.

HABITAT - in areas where water flows at least part of the year, such as streambanks, subalpine rivlets, wet meadows; 3,000-6,000 feet.

EDIBILITY - excellent. Brook Saxifrage is one of the few high mountain plants that provides good forage either raw or cooked. Use the young ·leaves in salads. The older ones are bitter and better used as a potherb.

Saxifraga comes from the Latin words 'saxum', rock, and 'frangere', to break, referring to the use of some species by herbalists in the treatment of "stones" of the urinary tract. *Arguta* means sharp-toothed, referring to the leaf margins. The common name is indicative of the habitat of Brook Saxifrage. Some common names are helpful in such a way while others are misleading.

drawing: Fall; ½x

Burdock

Burdock
Arctium minus (Hill) Bernh.
Composite Family - Compositae

FORM - a large leafed, biennial herb arising from a deep, fleshy taproot; a rosette of leaves the first year and an additional 3-5 feet tall flower stalk the second; the first year plant looks like rhubarb.

LEAVES - basal leaves egg-shaped to triangular, up to 18 inches long, with a heart-shaped base, long leaf stem, and wavy edges; stem leaves similar but reduced in size.

FLOWER - flower head of purplish flowers; July-Sept.

FRUIT - a burr, ¾ inch in diameter; Aug.-Oct.

HABITAT - widespread with varied habitat; pastures, vacant lots, fields; sea-level to mid elevations; a native of Eurasia that is well established here.

EDIBILITY - good. The deep taproot can be dug in June or July and cooked in vegetable dishes. Use the roots from the one year old plants. The roots tend to be woody if gathered after July and in the second year of growth. The Japanese use the root in some of their cookery. The young leaves are palatable only after 2 or 3 changes of boiling water. If the leaves are only cooked once, one is better off to throw the greens away and eat the pan.

The generic name, *Arctium*, probably is from the Greek word 'arktos' meaning a bear, referring to the rough texture of the burr. *Minus* means small and gives reference to this plant being smaller in stature than the Great Burdock.

The burrs of Burdock are what one may often find himself removing from the fur of his dog.

drawing: top to bottom, 2nd year Fall; ¼x, 1st year Summer; ⅛x

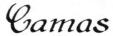

Camas

Camas
Camassia quamash (Pursh) Greene.
Lily Family - Liliaceae

The Camas was a plant held in high regard by the Indians of the Pacific Northwest. Camas fields were often tribal property and were protected as such. The bulb was used at feast times as a treat.

A cautionary note about Camas: It can easily be mistaken for a Death Camas, *Zigadenus*, which is highly poisonous. The two have many features in common, including similar habitats, bulbous rootstock, and tall grass-like leaves. If you fear mistaken identification of Camas, particularily when the plant is not in bloom, then wait until spring when it becomes simple to distinguish the blue flowering Camas from the cream colored Death Camas.

FORM - hyacinth-like herb; flower stalk taller than leaves; many growing together; deep, onion-like bulb 1-2 inches long.

LEAVES - basal; broadly linear (grass-like); 3-15 inches long.

FLOWER - blue-violet (rarely white); showy; 6-parted; many in a loose terminal cluster; individual flower star-like and 1½ inches across; flower stem a few inches taller than leaves; 6 yellow to blue anthers; April-June.

HABITAT - moist soils, at least in early spring; prairies; meadows, grassy flats, rocky areas; both sides of the Cascades; 1,000-2,500 feet.

EDIBILITY - good. The bulbous rootstock, which is somewhat slimy on the inside, is the part to eat, either boiled or roasted.

Camassia comes from the Indian name 'camas' or 'quamash'.

drawing: Spring; ¼x

Cattail
Typha latifolia L.
Cattail Family - Typhaceae

The Cattail is one of the primary plants for a forager to know. It is plentiful, widespread, easy to identify, many parts make good eating, and some part or other is useable the year around.

As may be apparent to some persons, the Cattail leaves and stalks make excellent weaving material. Among the Indians of western Washington the Cattail had greater value as a source for weaving material than as a source of food.

FORM - plants are 5-8 feet tall; mostly long leaves and flower stalk; many plants together; thick rootstock just below ground.

FLOWER - greenish; both male and female flowers in separate dense clusters; terminal male cluster above female cluster; each cone-like cluster is 3-7 inches long; May-June.

HABITAT – open, swampy areas; sea-level to 2,500 feet.

EDIBILITY – excellent. The starchy rootstock can be made into a flour by washing, roasting, and powdering it. This can then be used in the same way one would use any strong tasting flour. The rootstock can be gathered the year around if need be, but is best in the spring and summer. Spring and early summer are good times to harvest the succulent, inner stalk that is formed by the young leaf bases. To gather, simply pull up on the 3-4 innermost leaves. The leaf bases with the edible white center can be removed easily this way. Use them freshly sliced into salads or whole for nibbling. This is one of the finest wild taste treats. Both the male and female cone-like clusters can be boiled for 5-10 minutes, then buttered, seasoned, salted and eaten like corn on the cob (the inner stalk is too woody to eat). It's quite tasty! The clusters are best if obtained in May and early June, while the flowers are green or green-brown. After they have changed completely to brown, I find them not to be so good. When the male "cones" mature (June-July at sea-level), one can gather pollen to use as floavoring in soups or for a treat in breads.

Typha is the ancient Greek name for this plant. *Latifolia* means broad-leaved. This is compared to the narrow-leaved Cattail.

drawing: Summer; ½x

Chickweed

Chickweed
Stellaria media (L.) Cyrill.
Pink Family - Caryophyllaceae

Chickweed thrives in disturbed soils, like construction and destruction sites, or gardens. For this reason I refer to it as a 'people plant'. Surprisingly it lasts through cold spells that kill other annuals. This is the reason why in November or January one can find Chickweed and use it in salads. This is among the top of the wild edibles.

A word of caution is that there are many different Chickweeds. Although as far as I know none are poisonous, some are not pleasing to eat because of hairiness or a fibrous texture.

FORM - 5-12 inches high herbaceous 'weed'; very succulent stems and leaves; spreading stems, mat-forming; perennial in mild climates or annual in cold winters. One vertical line of hairs is located on the stem. It shifts about ¼ turn with each node. This is a particular characteristic of this Chickweed and helps to identify the plant.

LEAVES - opposite; egg-shaped in outline; ¾ inches long.

FLOWER - small white flowers in axils of leaves; inconspicuous; primarily April-June.

FRUIT - minute containers with shiny black seeds; primarily ripe in summer.

HABITAT - very widely spread; disturbed soils, sandy soils; open to partial shade; moist; vacant lots, flower gardens, vegetable gardens, along dirt roads, dirt compost piles, and country lawns; sea-level to 2,000 feet; considered a troublesome weed by many gardeners; native of Eurasia.

EDIBILITY - excellent. It is used raw in salads and cooked as a potherb or in soups. Try it in pancakes. Dried, it can be used to make a hot beverage or used in a biscuit mix to add flavor and color. Consider this one of the plants to know.

Stellaria refers to the star-shape of the small white flowers. The specific name, *media*, most likely refers to the fact that this Chickweed has characteristics between two other similar species.

drawing: Spring; 2x

Chocolate Lily

Chocolate Lily
Fritillaria atropurpurea Nutt.
Lily Family - Liliaceae

FORM - low growing perennial herb; 5-18 inches tall; deep bulbous rootstock with tiny rice-like bulblets.

LEAVES - generally 2; located near ground level; broadly linear; 2-6 inches long and up to 1 inch broad.

FLOWER - brownish-purple; spotted or mottled; ½-1 inch across; bell-shaped; 1-4 per flowering stalk; each hanging down.

HABITAT - sandy soils; prairies; sunny slopes or flat lands; sea-level to mountains.

EDIBILITY - good. The bulbous rootstock can be eaten raw or cooked lightly in a vegetable dish.

Yellow Bell, *Fritillaria pudica* (Pursh) Spreng., has one (rarely 2) yellow flower, is half as tall, and has 2 leaves. It is mainly found on the eastern side of the Cascades in sagebrush deserts, praires, and grasslands. Yellow Bell rootstock is eaten like that of Chocolate Lily.
Fritillaria comes from the Latin 'fritillus', dice box, in reference to the appearance of the capsule which holds the seeds. *Atropurpurea* means dark purple. *Pudica* means retiring and is used to describe the drooping flower which hides the reproductive parts.

drawing: left to right, Chocolate Lily, Summer; ½x, Yellow Bell, Summer; 1x

Chokecherry

Chokecherry
Prunus virginiana L.
Rose Family - Rosaceae

There are two types of Chokecherries, one on each side of the Cascades. The Chokecherry in western Washington has small hairs on the underside of the leaves, the other does not. The western version is apt to be shorter than its eastern relative, and bears less fruit.

Put this plant on your list of forage plants for several reasons. It has flavorful fruit; it is plentiful in eastern Washington and widespread in the western U. S.; when one finds a thicket of Chokecherries, there generally is enough fruit for several pints of jelly (even with leaving some for the birds and other wildlife).

FORM - 6-30 feet tall, commonly a 10 foot high tree; sometimes thicket-forming and sometimes tree-like with a trunk several inches in diameter; slightly reddish bark with short horizontal markings.

LEAVES - alternate; nearly egg-shaped; 1-2 inches long; finely toothed; 1 or 2 minute glands where the leaf blade and short, leaf stalk meet.

FLOWER - white; showy; numerous, small flowers in a 3-10 inch tall cluster; terminal clusters; May-June.

FRUIT - blackish-red when *ripe*; pea-sized; large pit; many hanging in a cluster; branches often drooping with the weight of the fruit; bitter tasting; Aug.-Oct.

HABITAT - semi-open area and often near stream banks; sea-level to 3,000 feet; plentiful in eastern Washington with a small number of plants in western Washington.

EDIBILITY - excellent. Eat the fruit only when fully ripe, for they contain a toxin when immature. The fruit makes an excellent jelly, especially when combined with apples.

Prunus comes from the ancient Latin name for plum, which is closely related to the cherries.

drawing: Fall; ¼ x

Curly Dock

Curly Dock
Rumex crispus L.
Buckwheat Family - Polygonaceae

FORM - erect, perennial herb from a deep, yellowish taproot; 1-3 feet tall at maturity.

LEAVES - basal leaves - leaf blade is lance-shaped and 3-10 inches long; crisp or wavy leaf margins; long leaf stem; stem leaves are similar to basal leaves, except reduced in size ascending the stem; both are bitter tasting (oxalic acid).

FLOWER - tiny, inconspicuous, greenish flowers form a dense cluster near the top of the top of the stem; June-August.

FRUIT - ⅛ inch long, 3-winged, brown fruit; July-Oct.; makes excellent dried flower arrangements.

HABITAT - widespread with varied habitats; fields, gardens, along paths, vacant lots; sea-level to mid elevations; native to Europe and is now well established in this and other areas of North America.

EDIBILITY - good. Use the young leaves, found in the early spring, after boiling for 5-10 minutes. They are mildly sour. These greens are high in vitamin A, containing twice that of Swiss chard and more than carrots. The ripe fruit can be gathered in the fall. The seeds can then be winnowed, ground, and used as a flour. This is a lot of work.

Rumex is the ancient Latin name used by Pliny, the Roman naturalist and writer who lived 23-79 A. D., for this group of plants. The specific name, *crispus*, refers to the wavy leaf margins.

drawing: Spring; ½x

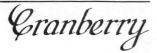

Cranberry

Currant and Gooseberry
Ribes species
Gooseberry Family - Grossulariaceae

Currants and Gooseberries are closely related, both have the genus *Ribes* in common. This genus is divided by common names into Gooseberries, which have tiny spines at the nodes and often on the internodes and fruit, and currants, which lack spines.

There are more than 2 dozen different kinds of these plants that grow in the Northwest. Some have greater flavor for jams, jellies, pies, and stuffings than others. I know of no *Ribes* that is poisonous, although some are very bitter.

East of the Cascades there are 2 Currants worth knowing. Squaw Currant, *Ribes cereum* Dougl., displays its olive green foliage from the sagebrush desert to mountain ridges. The leaves of this common shrub are fan-shaped, slightly lobed, and 1 inch across. The white to pinkish flowers, which start flowering in April, develop into the bright red fruit of July and August.

Golden Currant, *Ribes aureum* Pursh., blossoms yellow or orange during spring in the dry grasslands and the Ponderosa Pine forests. The shrub has leaves that are 3-lobed, ½-2 inches long, and distinctively yellow green. Young branches are reddish, while with age they change to dark gray. Late summer is the time to harvest the fruit, which can be either red, yellow, or nearly black. The extreme variability in fruit color suggests the same theme played by Salmonberry.

Squaw Currant and Golden Currant are best gathered when fully ripe, making an excellent wine at this time.

drawing: top to bottom, Squaw Currant, Summer; 1x, Golden Currant, Summer; 1x

Dandelion

Dandelion
Taraxacum officinale Weber.
Composite Family - Compositae

The Dandelion is familiar to most people so I will mention only a little about its description. The leaves of this perennial herb grow in a low rosette and are coarsely toothed. The hollow flower stem discharges a white milky juice when broken. The root is a thick taproot, much like that of a carrot.

The young leaves can be harvested in the spring or early summer. Use them raw in salads or cooked as a potherb. They are less bitter if they have been blanched, a process in which the leaves turn whitish. Blanching can be accomplished by putting some earth, a can or a board over your favorite Dandelion patch. The leaves, which are relatively high in vitamins A and C and in potassium, iron, and phosphorus, will be pale green in a couple of weeks. The leaves, young or old, can be gathered the year around to be dried and stored for use as a tea.

A hot beverage, frequently referred to as a coffee substitute, is prepared from the dried, roasted, and ground roots. The roots can be dug any time of the year. To make the hot drink, start with 2 tablespoons of ground roots and steep in a quart of boiled water. Another way is to put the coarsely ground material in a percolator and treat like coffee.

The cleaned, raw roots can also be sliced into salads or a pot of cooking vegetables.

A delicious wine can be prepared from the flower heads (use only the yellow part when making wine, don't get any greenery in). Try these yellow flowers in pancakes or fried into fritters.

Although the origin of the generic name, *Taraxacum*, is unclear, it may come from the Greek 'tarassein', to stir up, referring to the medicinal qualities of the Dandelion. *Officinale* means medicinal.

drawing: Spring—Fall; ¾x

English Plantain

English Plantain
Plantago lanceolata L.
Plantain Family - Plantaginaceae

   The Plantains are a troublesome weed to many gardeners, for they are invasive herbs. Several different Plantains are found in the Northwest. One should be able to find at least 2 types of this easily recognized plant on a casual walk around a yard, playfield, or pasture. Common Plantain, *Plantago major* L., has broadly elliptical leaves and is similar in most other respects to English Plantain.
   The Plantains rate only fair edibility in western Washington, because the leaves, except for the very young ones, are rather hairy and tough. I am told that where the winters are severe and the old foliage dies each year, the new leaves of spring are especially juicy and flavorful.

FORM - several leaves form a rosette with new leaves emerging from the center; last year's flower stalk often seen in the spring; tough perennial.

LEAVES - basal only; lance-shaped; 4-15 inches long; slightly hairy; several veins; tough with age.

FLOWER - greenish; not showy; dense clusters with many tiny flowers; 1-2 inch long cluster atop a 1-2 foot tall, leafless stem; 1 or many stems; April-Aug.

HABITAT - very wide spread herb; roadsides, pastures, lawns, gardens, vacant lots, pipe lines; most common west of the Cascades; native to Eurasia.

EDIBILITY - fair. The succulent leaves of the new year's growth are less hairy and leathery than the foliage of the previous year. These are the ones to use fresh in a salad or sandwich. The leaves can also be cooked, in which case one could use some of the tougher ones.

   Plantago comes from the Latin 'planta', the sole of the foot, descriptive of the leaf-shape of some Plantains. The specific name points out the characteristic lance-shape of the leaf of this specific plant.

drawing: top to bottom, English Plantain, Spring; ¾x, Common Plantain, Spring; ¾x

Evening Primrose

Evening Primrose
Oenothera biennis L.
Evening Primrose Family - Onagraceae

Since the choice part of the Evening Primrose is the large taproot of the first year plant, one needs to be able to tell it apart from the Foxglove, an extremely poisonous biennial that grows in similar habitats. It helps to know the characteristics of the Evening Primrose and to realize that the easily distinguished second year plant grows in the immediate locale. In other words, look for the 3-5 feet erect, leafy stem with bright yellow blossoms and the grey woolly leaves.

Mullein is another plant that could be confused for Evening Primrose. Mullein also is a biennial that has basal leaves which are very soft due to their wooliness, more so than Evening Primrose. The yellow flowers of Mullein are about ½ inch across and are in a tight, cone-like cluster.

FORM - stout biennial; rosette of leaves and a thick taproot the first year; rosette with a leafy, 2-5 feet erect stem emerging from the center the second year.

LEAVES - basal leaves are widely lance-shaped, 3-8 inches long, grey and wooly; stem leaves are lance-shaped and shorter.

FLOWER - clear yellow; showy; emerge from the axils of leaves; fragrant; 4 petals; 2 inches across the open blossom; short lived; June-Aug.

HABITAT - full sun; well drained soils, often sandy; open fields, vacant lots, along river banks; 1 and 2 year old plants grow together in localized clumps; sea-level to 2,000 feet.

EDIBILITY - good. The thick taproot of the 1 year old plant is the most edible portion. The cleaned root can be peeled or not and sliced to be cooked in soups, stews, stuffings, main dishes or any way you might use celery. Because of its peculiar flavor, use only a small portion, at least for your first taste.

Oenothera is the Greek name used by Theophrastus, the Greek philosopher and naturalist who lived about 300 B. C., to denote the Evening Primrose. *Biennis* means biennial, a term used to indicate that a plant germinates, grows, flowers, seeds, and dies in a period of 2 years. The showy, yellow flowers which produce a sweet fragrance open in the evening and from this comes the common name of Evening Primrose.

drawing: left to right, 2nd year Summer,
1st year Summer, 2nd year Summer; all ⅛x

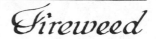

Fireweed

Fireweed (Willow Herb)
Epilobium angustifolium L.
Evening Primrose Family - Onagraceae

For the high elevation traveler of the Cascades, this plant is one to know for it is plentiful and provides good cooked forage. Although Fireweed is good food for some persons, it may cause allergic reactions to others. Eat only a small portion the first few times until you are certain that it is O.K. for you.

As early as March and April the young shoots are emerging from the earth. When they are about 6 inches tall they look like small willow trees. Also, look for the spent stalks from the previous year. The new shoots arise from their bases.

FORM - large perennial herb; dies back each fall; 3-8 feet tall; spike-like plant; often grows in large patches; immature Fireweed is easily mistaken for Pearly Everlasting or tiny Willow trees.

LEAVES - willow-like in shape (lance-shaped); averaging 3 inches long.

FLOWER - rose colored; many delicate flowers with 4 petals on a slender stalk; June-Sept.

HABITAT - generally full sun; well drained soils; logged forests, burned-over areas, moist banks, and roadsides; sea-level to alpine regions; extremely abundant plant west of the Cascades.

EDIBILITY - good. Use the young leaves and shoots as cooked greens. Although I have eaten the young shoots raw, their bitter taste is too much to make that a common practice. The dried leaves make an excellent hot beverage. The split stalk contains a mildly sweet glutinous substance suitable for soups or chewing on while hiking.

Epilobium comes from the Greek words 'epi', upon, and 'lobos', pod, referring to the inferior ovary. *Angustifolium* means narrow leaf. The name Fireweed can be used to remind oneself that this slender herb is one of the first to invade a burned area. Also, to some persons the color of the blossoms resembles the color of a fire.

drawing: left to right, Spring - Summer - Spring; ¼ x

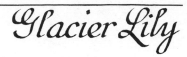

Glacier Lily (Dogtooth Violet)
Erythronium grandiflorum Pursh.
Lily Family - Liliaceae

FORM - delicate mountain plant; 4-18 inches tall; deep, bulbous rootstock; graceful plant that generally has 2 basal leaves and a single flowering stalk; great patches grow together.

LEAVES - 2 emerging from the stem at ground level; elliptical; 3-8 inches long; erect; veins running from leaf base to tip.

FLOWER - yellow; showy; 2-5 nodding flowers in a loose cluster; 1-2 inches across; 6 'petals'; April-May at 2,000 feet.

FRUIT - capsule; 1 inch long; 3 segments; July-Aug. at 2,000 feet.

HABITAT - sagebrush slopes to subalpine meadows; one of the first flowers to bloom after snow melt; not common in the Olympics; 2,000-7,000 feet.

EDIBILITY - good. The leaves, which have a slightly sweet taste, can be eaten raw or cooked. Cook only a few minutes in water. The bulbous rootstock can be eaten raw or cooked. However, it takes a lot of energy and patience to dig up the root, which easily breaks away from the slender flower stalk. For this reason it is advisable to selectively harvest only the leaves, taking only 1 from each plant.

The primary features that distinguish Avalanche Lily from Glacier Lily are mentioned below.

Avalanche Lily (Alpine Fawn Lily)
Erythronium montanum Wats.

FLOWER - white with a yellow center fading to pinkish with age; flowers point outward.

HABITAT - open to semi-open areas; above 3,000 feet west of the Cascades; found 2,000 feet and above east of the Cascades.

Erythronium comes from the Greek word 'erythro', red, referring to the pink *montanum* means pertaining to the mountains.

drawing: Glacier Lily, Spring - Summer; ¾x

Green Amaranth

Green Amaranth (Redroot, Pigweed)
Amaranthus retroflexus L.
Amaranth Family - Amaranthaceae

FORM - 2-5 feet tall annual herb with hairy stems; strong main axis with branches; a taproot, the upper part of which is red, especially noticeable when young.

LEAVES - alternately arranged; hairy on the lower surface, rough to the touch; 1-4 inch long leaf blade; leaf stem nearly as long as the blade; lance-shaped to egg-shaped; wavy edges.

FLOWER - greenish; 1-4 inch long clusters of numerous, inconspicuous flowers; July-Oct.

FRUIT - 1-3 inch long bristly cluster; minute shiny black seeds in cluster; Aug.-Oct.

HABITAT - widespread; rich sandy soils; vacant lots, gardens, along roadsides, along fence rows of agricultural fields; low elevations.

EDIBILITY - excellent. Eat the young shoots and leaves of spring and summer raw in salads or cooked as a solo vegetable or with other cooked greens, boiling for about 10 minutes. The fall leaves can be eaten after 15-20 minutes of boiling. The tiny seeds can be harvested in the fall, roasted and ground to produce a flour. This can then be used with a mixture of other flour for baking. This process takes much time and effort and may only be worth the novelty. Green Amaranth contains a high content of protein, calcium, phosphorus, and iron, more than either Spinach or Swiss Chard.

Amaranthus is derived from the Greek words 'a', meaning not, and 'marainein', meaning to wither or fade. This describes the resistance to wilting evident in Green Amaranth.

drawing: Summer or Fall; ½x

Harvest Lily

Harvest Lily
Brodiaea coronaria (Salisb.) Engl.
Lily Family - Liliaceae

The Harvest Lily is usually found growing singly or in small groups, unlike two of its relatives, Camas and Dogtooth Violet, which often carpet acres of open hills. Harvest Lilies can be most easily identified when the blue flowers dot the landscape of a prairie or a grassy hillside of eastern Washington. The flower stalks stand erect with no green leaves showing. At the base of the stalk is the flat-bottomed, 1 inch bulb.

FORM - simple looking perennial herb; solid bulb with papery outer coat.

LEAVES - basal; linear (grass-like); nearly equalling the flower stalk; drying before flowering.

FLOWER - blue with a white center; showy; 6-parted, several in a loose terminal looking cluster; radiating from 1 point; 5-12 inch erect flower stalk; June-July.

HABITAT - dry soils; open fields, grassy hillsides, prairies; primarily east of the Cascades.

EDIBILITY - good. Although I have eaten Harvest Lily only on a few occasions while visiting friends in the Okanogan foothills, I have found the raw bulbs to be tasty when consumed plain and in salads. The texture and flavor reminds me of a cross between celery and nut meat.

Brodiaea is named in honor of James J. Brodie, a Scotch botanist. *Coronaria* means used for or belonging to garlands.

drawing: Spring; ¾x

Hazelnut

Hazelnut
Corylus cornuta Marsh.
Birch Family - Betulaceae

In the early spring the characteristic clusters of male flowers hang from the leafless branches of the Hazelnut tree. At this time of the year it is easy to locate patches of Hazelnuts that have the potential to yield lots of good food. The harvest is a competitive one, with squirrels, chipmunks, and Stellar's Jays eating great quantities of the nut meat.

FORM - large shrub to tree-like; 10-25 feet tall; easily confused with the alder tree.

LEAVES - alternate; oval with rounded base and pointed tips; 2-4 inches long; finely toothed edge.

FLOWER - many tiny, male flowers in a 2-4 inch long, pendant cluster; 2 inconspicuous female flowers found at the branch ends; March-April.

FRUIT - 2 nuts ripen together; a papery 1¼ inch long outer shell covers the hazelnut; both the hazelnut and the meat inside the tough, brittle inner shell look like the commercial filbert; Aug-Oct.

HABITAT - thickets, pasture slopes, wood margins; primarily west of the Cascades.

EDIBILITY - excellent. Eat the nut any way you would use the store bought filbert, which is the horticultural development of the wild Hazelnut.

Corylus comes from the ancient Latin name for the Hazelnut. *Cornuta* means horned and refers to the papery shell on the fruit.

drawing: Fall; ½x

Highbush Cranberry

Highbush Cranberry (Squashberry)
Viburnum edule (Michx.) Raf.
Honeysuckle Family - Caprifoliaceae

This is one of the few plants on which fruit can be found during the lean winter and early spring months. At this time it is easy to identify, for the clusters of red fruit stand out on the leafless branches.

FORM - shrub to tree-like; up to 15 feet tall; difficult to locate in the underbrush during spring and summer.

LEAVES - opposite; 3 lobes with toothed margins; average 3 inches in diameter; purplish color in fall.

FLOWER - white; small flowers in a rounded, flat-topped cluster; cluster emerges from a short branch with only 2 leaves; May-July.

FRUIT - red or orange; berry-like; juicy; acidic; bitter; fruit in a cluster; 1 large flat seed; Aug.-Spring.

HABITAT - swamps to foothills; valleys, open woods, stream banks, and along coast; lowlands to mid elevations; not abundant in Washington.

EDIBILITY - fair. Use the fruit in winter and spring when it is fully ripe. In the fall when the fruit begins to ripen, it is very bitter. It can be used raw or cooked, perhaps best when cooked into jams or sauces.

Viburnum is the ancient Latin name for a plant in this genus. *Edule* refers to the fruit being edible.

drawing: Summer - Fall; ½x

Indian Plum

Indian Plum (Oso-berry)
Osmaronia cerasiformis (T. & G.) Greene.
Rose Family - Rosaceae

I have had difficulty finding the fruit of Indian Plum in any quantity beyond a few handfuls. This is probably due to at least 2 reasons. First, since only the plants that bear female flowers will have any fruit, the male plants are eliminated, or about half of the possible shrubs. The second reason is that the fruit develops early in the year and the birds quickly take advantage of the fresh food.

FORM - shrubby; clustered stems; 5-10 feet tall.

LEAVES - alternately arranged on the stem; widely lance-shaped and averages 3 inches long.

FLOWER - about a dozen small, white flowers on a drooping flower stem; the shrub is covered with color; rank-scented; male and female flowers on separate plants; one of the earliest of shrubs to flower after winter; Feb.-April.

FRUIT - blue-black when ripe, changing from an orange color; fleshy with a large flattened seed; the size of a pea; fruit on female plants only; May-July.

HABITAT - rich, moist soils; lowlands; a wide spread plant in western Washington.

EDIBILITY - excellent. Eat the fruit raw or cooked. Cooking reduces any bitter flavor. Use as with many berries. One has to beat the birds to the fruit.

Osmaronia comes from the Greek word 'osme' for smell or fragrant. This refers to the rank-scent of the flowers and the fragrance of the crushed foliage. The latter has a cucumber-like smell. *Cerasiformis* means cherry-form.

drawing: top to bottom, Spring - Late Summer; ¼x

Juneberry

Juneberry (Serviceberry, Shadbush, Sarviceberry)
Amelanchier alnifolia Nutt.
Rose Family - Roseaceae

The Serviceberry leaves and flowers are eaten by the deer, elk, mouse, mountain goats, rabbits, and rodents. It is one of the first shrubs to be eliminated or drastically retarded on overused ranges. Pheasants, grouse, and black bears eat the berries. During the winter the buds are staple food for the ruffed grouse.

FORM - 3-10 feet tall shrub or an 8-25 feet tall tree.

LEAVES - alternately arranged on the stem; ovalish (alder-shaped); 1-2 inches long; margin toothed at the tip or sometimes all around; 1-2 small glands at the leaf base.

FLOWER - white; about 1 inch in diameter; open bloom; May-June.

FRUIT - blue-black covered with a white waxy coat; pea-sized; apple-like in appearance; sweet and pulpy; July-Aug.

HABITAT - moist soil; open location; open fields at sea-level to partial forests at 4,500 feet.

EDIBILITY - excellent. Use the fruit raw, cooked or dried. Their flavor makes for fine pies or jams. A handful of fresh fruit can liven-up a bag of granola.
The fruit can be dried and used as a substitute for raisins or currants. The Indians pounded the fruit, spread out the mass and let it dry in large cakes for future use. It was also employed in making "pemmican". The Chehalis Indians used the dried berries as seasoning with meat and in soups.

The name Shadbush is from New England, where the plant blossoms during the annual run of shad. The specific name, *alnifolia*, refers to its alder-like leaves. The derivation of the generic name of *Amelanchier* is uncertain, although it is thought to be a French word.

drawing: top to bottom, Spring - Late Summer; 1x

Kinnikinnick

Kinnikinnick (Bearberry, Sandberry)
Arctostaphylos uva-ursi (L.) Spreng.
Heath Family - Ericaceae

For those persons interested in an effective, beautiful groundcover in their gardens and want to provide some native food for wildlife, this is an excellent plant to use, especially for sandy soils.

FORM - creeping, woody groundcover; 1-4 inches tall; red shredding bark on stems; rooting surface stems.

LEAVES - alternate; evergreen; shiny; oblong; 1 inch long; leathery.

FLOWERS - pink; inconspicuous; May-June.

FRUIT - red; pea-sized; white flesh; bland tasting; Aug.-Sept.; often lasting through the winter.

HABITAT - open hillsides and open forests; sandy soils; sea-level to 7,000 feet.

EDIBILITY - fair. Berries can be eaten raw, cooked or dried and ground. When eaten raw, the berries have a mealy texture and a bland taste. This improves when the fruit is added to other food. Dried leaves are used in smoking or as a tea substitute.

The naming system is a little redundant here. *Arctostaphylos* is from the Greek word 'arktos', meaning bear and 'staphyle', meaning bunch of grapes. The specific name, *uva-ursi*, is Latin for essentially the same. The Greek, Latin, and common names of Bearberry refer to the notion that bears consume the fruit, especially after hibernation. Many mammals and birds eat the colorful fruit of Kinnikinnick.

drawing: Fall; 1½x

Lamb's Quarters

Lamb's Quarters (Goosefoot, Pigweed)
Chenopodium album L.
Goosefoot Family - Chenopodiaceae

This plant should be put on the must list of Northwest foragers. It is widely spread, most often found where people are living (disturbed soils), and a rapid grower. Nearly all the parts of the plant are useable during one season or another. Furthermore, the flavor is one of the most enjoyable that I have found.

FORM - herbaceous annual; 2-3 feet tall at maturity (up to 6 feet in rich soil); main stem with many branches.

LEAVES - alternate; generally egg-shaped in outline although varying; 1-4 inches long; the older leaves more or less angularly toothed; the succulent leaves are unwettable, water beads off easily.

FLOWER - greenish or silvery when young; numerous in a terminal, open cluster; clusters expand up to 8 inches tall with maturity; June-Oct.

FRUIT - minute seeds in open terminal clusters; Sept.-Nov.

HABITAT - wide distribution; disturbed soils; rich soils; areas where people are (common plant of gardens and wastelands); native of Eurasia but naturalized in much of N. America.

EDIBILITY - excellent. The leaves can be used raw or cooked from spring to late fall. The younger the leaves, the more tender they are. I find the maximum cooking time is 5 minutes for young foliage. The flower buds and flowers make an excellent cooked dish. In the fall the seeds can be dried and ground into a flour or used unground over a salad or in bread as a flavor and texture change. The greens are relatively high in protein, compared with Spinach and Swiss Chard to which it is related.

Chenopodium comes from Greek 'chen', meaning goose, and 'podos', meaning foot. This refers to the leaf shape of some species. *Album* means white and is used to describe the color of the leaf undersurface.

This plant is sometimes called Pigweed, a name often applied to an entirely different plant that is called Green Amaranth in this book. A good example of the advantages of knowing the botanical name of a plant.

Mountain Sorrel

Mountain Sorrel
Oxyria digyna (L.) Hill.
Buckwheat Family - Polygonaceae

This is 1 of 3 plants that is described by the name Sorrel. The other 2 are Sheep Sorrel and Wood Sorrel. All contain the acrid tasting oxalic acid and all should be eaten only in small quantities.

FORM - grows in dense clumps; 6-15 inches tall with flower stalks taller than the leaves.

LEAVES - basal, kidney to heart-shaped; 1-2 inch broad leaf blade; 2-4 inch long leaf stalk; acrid, juicy; often tinged reddish.

FLOWER - green to reddish; borne on flower stalks; generally several flower stalks; July-Aug.

FRUIT - reddish; more conspicuous than the flowers; thin and flat; ¼-½ inch in diameter and indented at both ends; Sept.-Oct.

HABITAT - moist, rocky and gravelly locales; sometimes grows alone, often in shade of boulders; scree fields, rock crevices, and boulder patches; found only in subalpine and alpine regions.

EDIBILITY - excellent. The leaves and stems provide superior eating for the high country walker. They are filled with oxalic acid, the substance which produces the pleasantly acrid taste. Use the leaves as salad vegetables or cooked as a potherb. Remember not to eat too much of the plant, since large concentrations of oxalic acid can be harmful to the body. It's difficult to say what is too much, but eating a couple dozen leaves during a day certainly has been refreshing for me with no ill effects.

Oxyria comes from the Greek language and means sour, in reference to the taste of the leaves.

drawing: Fall; ¼x

Mustard

Mustard
Brassica species
Mustard Family - Cruciferae

I have treated *Brassica* in general, because there are many members of this genus which are edible but difficult to tell apart. It includes such "weeds" as Black Mustard, Charlock, White Mustard, Leaf Mustard, and Field Mustard. These have been introduced from Europe and Asia. This genus is an important agricultural one, containing broccoli, brussels sprouts, cabbage, cauliflower, mustard, kale, rutabaga, and turnip.

FORM - annuals or perennials; 2-4 feet tall with course, large leaves; erect main axis with branches; root varies in shape from a thickened taproot to a slender turnip.

LEAVES - basal leaves laterally lobed and averaging 6 inches in length; stem leaves are reduced in size and less lobed ascending the stem; all leaves clasp the stem.

FLOWER - generally yellow and colorful; many ½ inch diameter flowers bloom ascending the stem; 4 petals per bloom; several flower stalks per plant; primarily May-June.

FRUIT - many slender, 1-2 inch long capsules on a stalk; fruit developes while flowers are still opening further up the stalk; peppery-hot tasting; June-Aug.

HABITAT - moist soils; full sun; waste lands, vacant lots, field edges, abandoned gardens; low elevations.

EDIBILITY - excellent. The young leaves can be eaten raw. As the leaves grow older they are best used cooked, for they get tough with age. Boil or steam the leaves as you would the commercial Mustard greens. They are good cooked alone, in conjunction with other greens, or in soups. When eaten fresh the slender taproot has a hot peppery taste. It is pleasant enough to use in thin slices for salads. The roots could be used to add a flavorful touch to cooked dishes. Use a piece of the root 2 inches long for each person. The seeds have the strongest flavor of all parts of the Mustard plant. Use either the fresh or dried seeds as a spice on meat or in soups. The seeds contain an oil which causes irritation to some persons.

drawing: Spring; ¾x

Oregon Grape

Oregon Grape
Berberis aquifolium Pursh.
Barberry Family - Berberidaceae

FORM - 2-10 feet tall; shrubby; many stems from a clump.

LEAVES - pinnately compound; shiny; evergreen, although often turning to orange-purple in the fall and winter; 3-12 inches long; 5-7 leaflets with 1 major vein at each leaflet base; leaflets are holly-like, having spiny teeth.

FLOWER - yellow; numerous in a rather tight, 3-10 inch long, terminal cluster; April-June.

FRUIT - blue berries; clusters just below present year's growth; waxy, whitish coat; acidic; about pea-sized; Aug.-Oct.

HABITAT - forests and open areas; abundant fruit bearing plants grow in the sun; lowlands to mountains.

EDIBILITY - excellent. Eat the fruit raw or cooked. It makes excellent jams and preserves. Use with Salal to make a jelly. Use the berries in teas for flavoring or in bird stuffing. The very young, copper-colored leaves are pleasantly bitter tasting when eaten fresh. The flowers are, also, edible in small quantities. Good plant to know.

Low Oregon Grape or Long-leaved Oregon Grape, *Berberis nervosa*, is a similiar species. The main differences are:

FORM - 10-24 inches tall; in the young plants the leaves emerge from a more or less central point at the base; underground runners.

LEAVES - 10-30 inches long; 9-15 leaflets, each with 3 major veins at the base.

Berberis is from the Arabic name, 'berberys', for this genus of plants. The specific name, *nervosa*, refers to the prominent veins seen in the leaflets. *Aquifolium* means holly-leaf, coming from the Holly Family, Aquifoliaceae.

drawing: left to right, Fall - Spring; ¾x

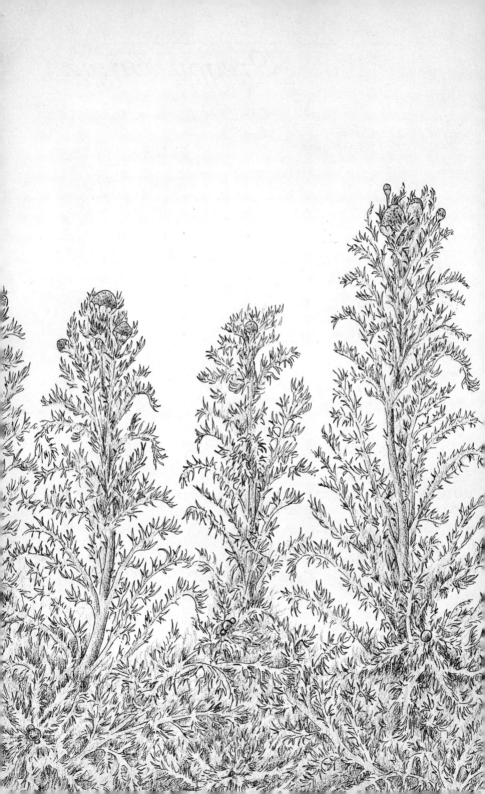

Pineapple Weed

Pineapple Weed (Chamomile, also spelled Camomile)
Marticaria matricariodies (Less.) Porter.
Composite Family - Compositae

This "weed" grows nearly everywhere in the cities and towns of this region. Once you are able to identify Pineapple Weed, you will be surprised at its widespread destruction. It thrives in poor, hard-packed soils, such as along paths, free growing lawns, and vacant lots. It also can be found in such unlikely places as cracks in sidewalks and hard gravel parking lots. This plant grows where people live and work.

From June to September the flower heads can be picked from the plant. They dry quickly when placed on a screen. When dry, they are ready to be stored for use as one of nature's winter beverages. Keep the flower parts and the leaves separate, because the flavor of the latter is overpowering and for most persons disagreeable.

This plant is different from Chamomile, *Anthemis* species, that is frequently sold as an herb in some indoor plant shops. Chamomile has small white petals surrounding the yellow flower. It is not native to this area.

FORM - 3-15 inches tall, commonly only a few inches high; "weedy" annual or perennial; pineapple-scented to some persons.

LEAVES - ½-2 inches long; 1-3 times divided and feathery looking.

FLOWER - light yellow flower heads; conical; pea-sized; flower head appears to lack 'petals'; numerous, terminal heads; aromatic; June-Sept.

HABITAT - full sun; poor or hard-packed soil; cracks of side-walks, gravel parking lots, along paths; lowlands.

EDIBILITY - excellent!! The dried flower heads produce a pleasing aroma, described by some as that of a pineapple. 1 heaping teaspoon of flowers makes 1 quart of tea. I have eaten biscuits that have had Pineapple Weed added to the dough for flavor. They were simply great.

Matricaria is the name given by herbalists a few hundred years ago to herbs of reputed medicinal value.

drawing: Spring - Fall; 1x

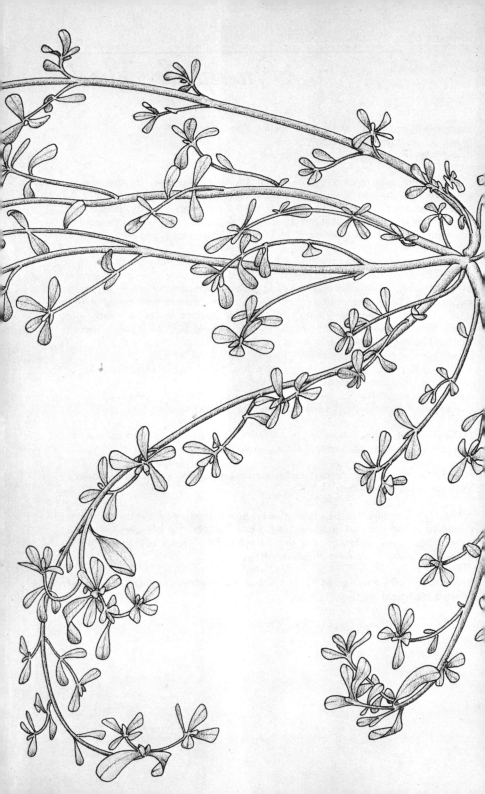

Purslane

Purslane (Pussley)
Portulaca oleracea L.
Purslane Family - Portulacaceae

Purslane has been eaten in India and Persia for more than 2,000 years and used in Europe and Asia as a garden vegetable for many generations.

FORM - succulent, fleshy annual; several horizontal or sprawling branches, up to 10 inches long; plant rarely more than 1 inch tall, looking like a groundcover.

LEAVES - alternately arranged, flattened, thick leaves; ½-1 inch long.

FLOWER - yellow; minute flowers in the axils of leaves or small terminal clusters; June-Fall.

FRUIT - black seeds; minute; 10-12 weeks after flowering.

HABITAT - rich, moist and disturbed soils; full to partial sun; gardens, vacant lots, fields; lowlands; native to southern Europe is now well established in this country.

EDIBILITY - excellent. The leaves and stems of the plant can be gathered from spring until the first killing frosts. The young shoots and leaves can be used raw, cooked, or pickled. The raw plant has a slightly slimy feel when the leaves or stems are crushed. As a cooked vegetable, wash well and steam for 5-10 minutes. As with gathering many greens, one need only harvest some of the leaves or shoots, rather than the entire plant. This way, one has a source of fresh greens later in the year. Purslane contains a high percentage of iron and calcium, more than either Spinach or Swiss Chard.

The derivation of the generic name is obscure. However, *Portulaca* is the name used by Pliny, the Roman naturalist and writer (23-79 A.D.), to denote this plant or one closely related.

drawing: Summer; 1x

Salal

Salal
Gaultheria shallon Pursh.
Heath Family - Ericaceae

As a wild food source the Salal fruit is one of the most valuable in the Northwest for humans and other wildlife. The Indians recognized this fact by mashing the berries and drying them into cakes, sometimes weighing as much as 10 to 15 pounds. Salal is abundant, easy to identify, and the fruit is excellent. This is a plant that needs to be near the top of any foragers list of edibles. Many birds and mammals eat the fleshy fruit.

FORM - shrubby 2-8 feet tall; dense thickets along the coast; often in the form of thick underbrush 2-4 feet high.

LEAVES - alternate; evergreen; egg-shaped in outline; rough textured and glossy; 2-4 inches long; leathery.

FLOWER - whitish-pink; a loose cluster with flowers hanging down; May-July.

FRUIT - purplish-black; berry-like; opening opposite the stem; larger than the size of a pea; Aug.-Oct.

HABITAT - forests or open area; sea-level to 4,000 feet; very common west of the Cascades.

EDIBILITY - excellent. The fruit is used raw as trail food or cooked as preserves.

Gaultheria is named in honor of Jean Francois Gaultier, 1708-1756, physician and botanist of Quebec. The common name, Salal, is derived from an Oregon Indian name for the plant.

drawing: Fall; ¾x

Salmonberry

Salmonberry
Rubus spectabilis Pursh.
Rose Family - Rosaceae

Salmonberry and Thimbleberry are often confused. This apparently has to do with the fact that both grow in a nearly identical habitat and are similar in general outline when the plants are not in flower.

An interesting etymological possibility for Salmonberry has to do with the astringent bark being a remedy for digestive disorders caused by eating too much salmon, a malady peculiar to the Northwest. Also the name identifies the color of some of the fruit.

FORM - erect, thicket-forming shrub with brown bark; 4-8 feet tall; stems armed with weak prickles.

LEAVES - 3 leaflets per leaf; leaflets ovalish, often lobed, with toothed margins.

FLOWER - deep pink; showy; solitary; 1½ inches in diameter; 5 petals; March-April.

FRUIT - red to salmon-colored; raspberry-like; mildly sweet; June-July.

HABITAT - open fields to forest borders; stream banks, fence rows, underbrush; sea-level to 3,000 feet; primarily west of the Cascades; abundant in Puget Sound region.

EDIBILITY - excellent. The berries are good raw or cooked. The cooked fruit can be used in pies, tarts, and preserves. Hot Salmonberry pie and ice cream is worth a try. The dried leaves can be steeped for a hot beverage.

Rubus is the ancient Latin name for a member of this genus. The specific name, *spectabilis*, refers to the showy display of the flower.

Primary differences between Salmonberry and the closely related Thimbleberry:

Thimbleberry
Rubus parviflorus Nutt.

LEAVES - large (6 inches across) leaves with 5 lobes, maple-like.

FRUIT - red and hemispherical rather than raspberry-like in shape.

FLOWER- white; April-May.

HABITAT - sea-level to 4,500 feet.

Parviflorus means small-flowered.

drawings: top, Salmonberry Summer; ½x
bottom, Thimbleberry Summer; ½x

Sheep Sorrell

Sheep Sorrel (Red Sorrel, Dock)
Rumex acetosella L.
Buckwheat Family - Polygonaceae

Sheep Sorrel should be one of the first plants you learn for a couple of reasons. It is easy to identify because of the characteristic arrow-shaped, basal leaves and the bitter taste of the stem and leaves. The plant is green and useable during all except the severe winter months. Sheep Sorrel is an herb that is useful in cookery, except one should not eat large amounts due to the high concentration of oxalic acid. I've sampled a variety of soups that used Sheep Sorrel and found all delicious. The directions for making one of these soups is in the recipe section.

FORM - perennial herb; a cluster of basal leaves in spring; in summer a flowering stem up to 20 inches tall; in fall a stem with seeds and a few basal leaves; spreads rapidly by slender underground rootstocks.

LEAVES - basal leaves are arrow-shaped and 1-2 inches long; the stem leaves are lance-shaped and smaller in size; both are sour tasting.
FLOWER - small, numerous, reddish flowers on a long flower stalk; flower cluster erect, open, and not obvious, except in mass; April-June.

HABITAT - open areas with disturbed soils and undisturbed soils; sandy soils; along roadways, in gardens, along telephone and power line rights of way in the country, in yards, and logging roadheads; sea-level to 3,000 feet; considered a troublesome weed by many gardeners; native to Europe.

EDIBILITY - excellent. Refreshing when eaten raw, especially in salads and sauces. It cooks well in soups, or used as a cooked green to improve the bland taste of some vegetables. I enjoy a couple dozen leaves of Sheep Sorrel cooked with a serving of Nettles. The bitter taste of the leaves and stems is due to oxalic acid. Dried leaves make a tea. The fresh leaves can also be made into a cold drink.

Rumex was the ancient Latin word for this plant.

drawing: Spring; 1x

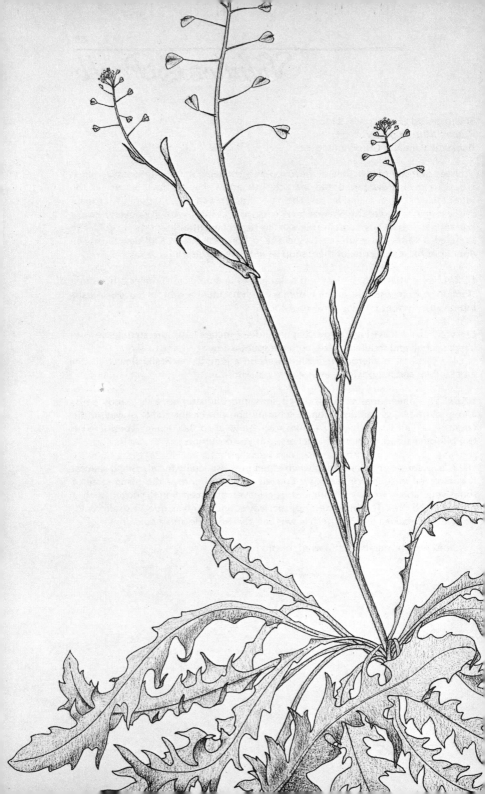

Shepherd's Purse

Shepherd's Purse
Capsella bursa-pastoris (L.) Medic.
Mustard Family - Cruciferae

FORM - a cluster of basal leaves form early on the annual; "weedy" looking plant; tiny leaves on flower stalk.

LEAVES - basal leaves are widely lance-shaped, 2-3 inches long, generally deeply lobed; stem leaves are smaller, lance-shaped and clasp the stem.

FLOWER - white; not showy; tiny blooms on the stalk that flower near the top as the 4-15 inch stem elongates; March-July.

FRUIT - characteristically triangular; many fruits on the stem while the plant is still flowering; 2 months after flowering.

HABITAT - rich soils; disturbed soils; waste places, gardens, fields; widely distributed; regarded as a weed by gardeners; introduced from Europe.

EDIBILITY - good. Use the young leaves, particularly if they have been blanched, in salads or cooked as a potherb. A friend has mentioned using the seeds for sprouting. I'm not sure of her success. The Indians ground the dried seeds into a meal, this however would require a tremendous amount of patience and effort.

The fruit is described by the botanical name in two different ways. *Capsella* means a little box, for the fruit is a container that holds the seeds. More than 200 years ago someone's imagination carried him to the point of relating the fruit's shape to a "shepherd's purse", *bursa-pastoris*.

drawing: Summer; 1x

Shooting Star

Shooting Star (Bird Bill)
Dodecatheon species
Primrose Family - Primulaceae

There are about half a dozen different species of Shooting Star in the Northwest. All are similar, comprised of a rosette of leaves, a leafless flower stalk, and striking blossoms that have reflexed petals. The height of the plant, the flower number and color are the main differences among the types.

For the high country hiker this is a plant to recognize and use. However, selective harvesting is the key to a continuing population of Shooting Stars. This striking herb could easily be eliminated from an area with careless gathering.

FORM - showy, perennial herb when in flower; rosette of leaves with a single flowering stem emerging from the center.

LEAVES - basal; few to several; roundish-oblong leaf blade with a short leaf stalk; 2-5 inches long; generally smooth edges.

FLOWER - reddish, violet, white, pinkish; showy; few to several flowers in a loose, terminal cluster; leafless flower stem that is 5-18 inches tall; April-June.

HABITAT - moist soils; full or partial sun; prairies, along streams, subalpine meadows; both sides of the Cascades; sea-level to 7,000 feet.

EDIBILITY - good. The leaves, stems, and flowers can be eaten raw or cooked. The flowers in a salad will cause a bit of excitement and be a topic of conversation.

Dodecatheon comes from the Greek 'dodeka', 12, and 'theos', god, for the plant was protected by the Greek gods.

drawing: Spring - Summer; 1x

Siberian Miner's Lettuce

Siberian Miner's Lettuce (Miner's Lettuce)
Montia sibirica (L.) Howell.
Purslane Family - Portulacaceae

There are 12 species of Miner's Lettuce found in the Pacific Northwest. Many of them appear similar. Although I have tried only 4 (all good tasting), I expect that the others could be just as acceptable. I know of no *Montia* that is poisonous.

FORM - very succulent herb with a slender taproot; many flower stems and basal leaves arise from 1 central location; often straggly form reaching 4-12 inches tall; a perennial in mild climates.

LEAVES - basal leaves broadly lance-shaped to egg-shaped, 1-2 inch long blade with a long leaf stem; 2 opposite stem leaves, egg-shaped, 1-2 inches long, and no leaf stem; reddish cast in winter.

FLOWER - white to deep pink; open cluster of many small flowers; 2-5 inch long cluster; 5 notched petals; March-Sept.

HABITAT - rich sand or gravel soils; moist conifer forests; partial shade; lowlands to 3,000 feet; extremely abundant in western Washington.

EDIBILITY - excellent. One of the best plants to eat raw. Leaves, stems, and flowers can be eaten. Use in salads or as a trail snack. If used as a cooked green, steam only for 1-2 minutes.

Montia is named in honor of Guiseuppe Monti, 1682-1760, an Italian botanist. The specific name, *sibirica*, is used because it was in Siberia that the plant was first sighted (1753) and then described in botanical literature. The common name, Miner's Lettuce, comes from the past traditional usage. Miners, particularly from the era of 1849, used the foliage as a substitute for their "back home" lettuce.

The main differences between the two similar species is cited below.

FORM - 2-8 inches tall; annual.

LEAVES - basal leaves uniformly wide and lance-shaped, 1-3 inch long blade with a long leaf stem; 2 opposite stem leaves appearing as one round leaf surrounding the stem (sometimes twice notched and-or twice pointed), 1-2 inches broad.

FLOWER - loose cluster of several small flowers; March-July.

HABITAT - not as abundant as Siberian Miner's Lettuce.

Perfoliata refers to the fact that the stem perforates what appears to be a single, disk-shaped, stem leaf.

drawings: top, Miner's Lettuce Spring; ¾x
bottom, Siberian Miner's Lettuce Spring; ¾x

Springbeauty

Springbeauty
Claytonia lanceolata Pursh.
Purslane Family - Portulacaceae

Springbeauty is an appropriate common name for this delightful herb. It is one of the first subalpine plants to emerge after the cold dormancy of winter and to cheer the mountain traveler. Often large patches can be seen growing near drainage from snowbanks.

The delicate Springbeauty is one that feeds my visual appetite as well as my stomach when in the high country. I always look for these plants, because they provide my favorite salad material. I have found that I have needed to develop a taste for some of the wild flavors, but this was not the case with Springbeauty. The succulent leaves are pleasant tasting, while the stems and flowers are edible also.

Find yourself a short stick and start digging after a few of the rootstocks. You will need to go about 6 inches to get the starch bulb. It will take work, but 1 or 2 dozen in a noodle dish will furnish a nutritional addition to dinner and a memorable treat to your outdoors experience.

Some botanists place Springbeauty in the genus *Montia* (Miner's Lettuce). This is done because the flowers and leaves are strikingly similiar. However, Springbeauty has a bulbous rootstock, not a fibrous one like the *Montias*. The *Claytonia* is also an upland cousin, being found only in mountainous regions.

FORM - 3-6 inch tall perennial herb; semi-round rootstock, like that of a garden gladiolus but ½-1 inch in diameter; 1 or several stems from one rootstock.

LEAVES - 1 or 2 basal leaves in spring and early summer, each having a 2-4 inch long, lance-shaped leaf blade; the 2 opposite, 1-3 inch long stem leaves are slender and occur partly above and partly below ground.

FLOWER - white, often with some pink veins; showy; 1 or several in an open cluster; 3-10 inch tall flower stalk; May-July.

HABITAT - open to semi-protected; found near melting snowbanks early in the summer; sagebrush foothills, open fields, subalpine meadows; both sides of the Cascades; 3,000-7,000 feet.

EDIBILITY - excellent. The entire plant can be eaten cooked or raw. The raw bulb is crunchy and flavorful in dishes with fresh or cooked vegetables. The foliage and flowers are of top quality.

Claytonia is in honor of John Clayton, 1685-1773, a botanist who collected chiefly in the eastern United States. *Lanceolata* refers to the lance-shaped leaves.

drawing: Spring - Summer; 1x

Stinging Nettle

Stinging Nettle
Urtica dioica L.
Nettle Family - Urticaceae

Although the young leaves do not tend to sting as much as the more mature ones, the sensation is not a pleasant one. Use gloves when picking the Nettle. When one touches the leaves the tips of the sharp, hollow hairs penetrate the skin and break, depositing the toxin. The result is painful burning or stinging along with a localized rash. Depending upon one's sensitivity, this lasts for a couple hours or a couple days. To reduce the pain I have at one time or other rubbed the leaves of Bracken Fern, Horsetail, and Thimbleberry on the painful area. All produced relief for a period of 10 minutes to an hour. The stinging quality was employed by the Quileute seal hunters, for they would rub themselves with the Nettles before going out to sea. This was done to help them stay awake through the night.

The western Washington Indians used the Nettle for other purposes. The leaves, stems, and roots were used medicinally. A tonic was prepared from any or all of the forementioned to reduce the pain and discomfort of rheumatism, colds, headaches, and childbirth.

FORM - a perennial herb with a single straight stem; 2-8 feet tall; spreading rootstocks create large patches; plants often grow in gatherings; stem 4-sided; all parts armed with stinging hairs.

LEAVES - opposite; numerous; egg-shaped to heart-shaped; 2-6 inch long leaf blade; leaf stem ½ to ⅛ the blade length; coursely toothed; dark green; dried foliage with a strong oder.

FLOWER - greenish; numerous minute flowers that form a drooping auxiliary cluster; several per plant; May-June.

HABITAT - in deep rich soil or near moisture, frequently shady; sea-level to 5,000 feet; extremely abundant in the Pacific Northwest.

EDIBILITY - excellent. *Use only after cooking or drying.* Steam the young shoots, which are high in iron, protein, and citamin C, for 3-5 minutes and serve with butter, salt, pepper, and something acidic, like lemon juice or Sheep Sorrel leaves. The most succulent and tasty foliage is gathered in the spring when the plant is less than 1 foot tall. Simply pick the top shoot of 4-6 leaves. The pinkish-white rootstock is edible and can be used to make soup stock.

Urtica comes from the Latin word 'uro', to burn, because of the stinging hairs on the Nettle. *Dioica* means that the male and female flowers are on separate plants. In general this is not true with the Nettles that are found in the Northwest.

drawing: Spring through Summer, ½x

Stonecrop

Stonecrop
Sedum species
Stonecrop Family - Crassulaceae

There are more than half a dozen Sedums in the foothills and mountains of the Pacific Northwest, including 2 that have rose-colored flowers. The distinctions among species are based primarily on technical features.

It is interesting to note that the leaves of this succulent plant are covered by a waxy substance. This inhibits evaporation of moisture and enables the plant to survive in dry weather and soil. During this time Stonecrop goes into a state of reduced growth, only to snap into a flush of growth when the water is again available.

FORM - looks like a typical rock garden plant; low growing fleshy leaves; perennial.

LEAVES - basal leaves are small, roundish and tightly clustered; the stem leaves are ½-1 inch long and lance-shaped to disk-shaped; both are succulent and thick; sometimes grey green.

FLOWER - yellow and showy; many clustered together to terminate a 1-4 inch tall flower stalk; May-July.

HABITAT - sandy to rocky soils; full sun; most are middle to high elevation dwellers.

EDIBILITY - good. The leaves are the best part of the plant, although the brilliant yellow flowers add a touch of color to a bland dish of freeze dried food. Use the foliage raw or cooked. The mucilaginous leaves, which contain an unusually large amount of water, tend to quench ones thirst. Limit your eating to a few tablespoons worth. A few years ago I was hiking with a person who "went bananas" over the idea that Stonecrop could be eaten. He ate about 2 cups of the fresh leaves and became nauseated within a short time.

Sedum comes from 'sedeo', to sit, referring to the plant's squatty appearance.

drawing: Summer; 1x

Thistle

Thistle
Cirsium species
Composite Family - Compositae

FORM - stout biennial or perennial herbs; 1-6 feet tall; a stalk up to 2 inches in diameter; covered with soft or stiff hairs; hollow stem.

LEAVES - leaves alternately arranged or basal; coursely toothed and deeply lobed; sharp marginal prickles; 1-8 inches long.

FLOWER - white, pink, and reddish-purple; large spiny looking flower heads; June-July.

FRUIT - seeds on the end of a parachute of silky hairs (same as with the Dandelion); fruit head composed of spines; the seeds are a favorite food of the American Goldfinch; July-Sept.

HABITAT - side spread plant; full sun to partial shade; meadows, roadsides, gardens, and vacant lots; sea-level to 4,000 feet.

EDIBILITY - good. The young stalks when gathered before flowering are the most succulent. Split the stalk and eat the mildly sweet inside. Simply use your knife or teeth to scrape the inner surface of the hollow stem. If the outer hairs are removed, the stalk can be cut into sections and cooked as celery. The flavor and texture of young plants is pleasing and well worth eating. I have eaten the oversized taproot. After cleaning it completely, I sliced sections into a vegetable (tomato base) soup. There wasn't much flavor change to the soup, but the crunchy texture of the Thistle root was pleasant.

Cirsium comes from the Greek word for this plant 'kirsion'. It means a swollen vein. The Thistle was reputed to be a remedy for this condition.

drawing: Spring; 1x

Violet

Violet
Viola species
Violet Family - Violaceae

There are a large number of different violets, varying in plant height, leaf size, and flower color. They all are, however, similar enough to remind one of a small pansy without a face.

I find the leaves of most Violets slightly hairy and tough when eaten fresh. For this reason I use them with other greens, as in a salad, or cooked, where they lose some of their undesirable qualities.

FORM - a low perennial herb; 1-15 inches tall, commonly only a few inches high.

LEAVES - often evergreen; heart-shaped; 1-3 inches long; some species have long leaf stems.

FLOWER - shite, yellow, purple, and bluish; sometimes flowering in the fall as well as spring; 5 petals; generally March-June.

HABITAT - full to partial sun; moist to dry soils; a wide spread plant in terms of elevation and location; forests, country lawns, prairies; sea-level to 5,000 feet.

EDIBILITY - good. The leaves can be used raw in the spring for salads, or picked any time of the year and dried to be used as a hot beverage, or added to soups. They are high in vitamins C and A. The flowers make a colorful addition to gelatin salads or desserts.

drawing: Spring; 3x

Water Cress

Water Cress
Rorippa nasturtium- aquaticum (L.) Schinz & Thell.
Mustard Family - Cruciferae

Be absolutely sure of the identification of Water Cress! Why? The deadly poisonous Water Hemlock (page 145) grows in the same kind of wet, marshy, stream areas. The greatest danger is that Water Hemlock could be mistaken for the delicious Water Cress in the early spring, especially by a novice. Water Hemlock is not simply toxic, but is highly poisonous.

FORM - herbaceous water plant; trailing stems with only tips erect; 3-15 inches tall; free floating branches, rooting easily at nodes.

LEAVES - young leaves entire; mature leaves are 3-12 inches long with 3-11 lateral segments and a large terminal lobe; peppery taste to the leaves and stems.

FLOWER - minute blooms form a white cluster, 1-2 inches across; April-July.

FRUIT - 1 inch long slender capsule; hot peppery taste; June-Aug.

HABITAT - slow moving water; many of the creeks and streams of the Northwest; grows with the tiny Duckweed and the poisonous Water Hemlock; sea-level to 2,500 feet; native to Europe.

EDIBILITY - excellent. One of the most refreshing tastes in the wild. Just because Water Cress grows in the water, it is incorrect to assume that the water in drinkable. Likewise, be sure the water is free of pollutants before eating it. Use the stems, leaves, and fruit fresh as in salads. Try a cheddar cheese sandwich with the leaves. It can be cooked or dried and used as a spice, which can be used as a pepper substitute.

Rorippa is said to be derived from 'rorippen', the Saxon common name for the plant. One will sometimes find *Nasturtium officinale* as the scientific name for Water Cress.

drawing: Spring - Fall; 1x

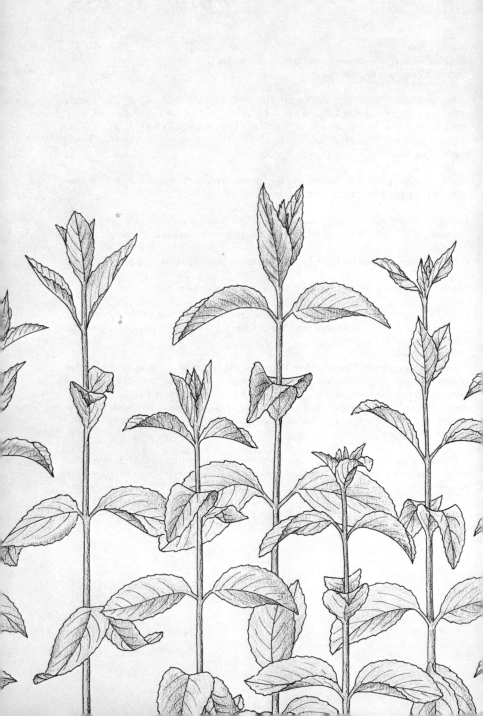

Wild Mint

Wild Mint
Mentha species
Mint Family - Labiatae

There are at least 4 different Wild Mints that can be found in the Pacific Northwest. All are very similar in appearance, having square stems, oppositely arranged leaves, and foliage with a characteristic mint odor. There is no difference between the garden varieties and those that are found in the wilds. The Mints were originally introduced from Europe and have escaped from cultivation in the United States.

All Mints thrive in moist, rich soils. Favorite locations are along streams, ditches, and shores, bottom lands, and moist grasslands. It is even common to find Wild Mint growing in a stream in much the same manner that Water Cress does.

The Mints make some of the finest teas. Use the dried leaves and stems alone or in conjunction with such tea plants as Rose hips, Pineapple Weed flower heads, and Strawberry leaves.

drawing: Spring-Summer; ½x

Wild Onion

Wild Onion
Allium species
Lily Family - Liliaceae

There are many types of Wild Onions, differing in plant height, flower clusters and colors, habitat, and other features. When gathering Wild Onions, it is necessary to be certain of their identification, for this plant looks much like Death Camas and Mt. Death Camas. As one might imagine the latter 2 are fatally poisonous. A successful way of determining the identity of Wild Onions is by their odor. If the plant smells like an Onion, it is! If the plant *does not* smell like an Onion, even with crushing the stem, flowers, or bulb, then it *is not*.

FORM - aromatic perennial herb with an underground bulb, ½ inch in diameter; few to many grass-like leaves.

LEAVES - basal; linear in shape, flat or hollow, and up to 20 inches tall; leaves frequently wither before flowering.

FLOWER - white, pinkish, or purple; many small flowers in a cluster; clusters either dense or open and either upright or nodding; May-Aug.

HABITAT - moist to dry soils; full to partial sun; grows in meadows, on hillsides, near seasonal streams; sea-level to 6,000 feet.

EDIBILITY - excellent. The Wild Onion can be used in the same ways one would use the store bought onion. The flavor of the native Onion, however, may be considerably stronger. Some of the dried Wild Onion bulbs have a flavor as potent as garlic. In some species the fresh flowers have a stronger taste than the fresh bulbs.

'Alum' is the name that was used in ancient Rome for garlic, hence the generic name of *Allium*.

drawing: Spring - Summer; 1x

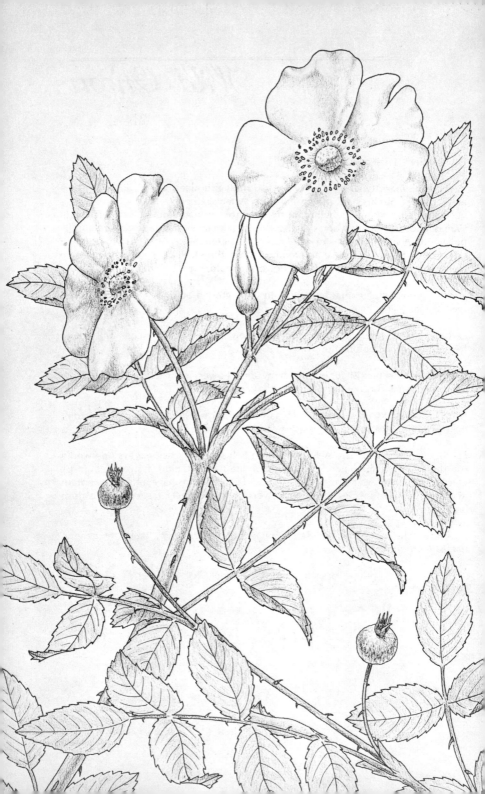

Wild Rose
Rosa species
Rose Family - Rosaceae

There are about half a dozen different species of Rose that occur in the Northwest. All the hips look much alike and all are edible.

This is an excellent plant to become familiar with if you are interested in making winter teas or supplementing your vitamin C intake. Dried and finely ground rose hips add a mildly sweet flavor to hot beverages made from Fireweed, Pineapple Weed, Strawberry leaves, and Mint. I have even used Rose hips with the potent leaves of Nettle and had good results.

FORM - 2-7 feet tall; erect shrub with thorns.

LEAVES - alternate; pinnate; 5-9, ovalish leaflets; 2 rows of teeth on the margins.

FLOWER - pink; 2-3 inches in diameter; solitary; fragrant; May-June.

FRUIT - bright red or orangish; called a hip; pea-sized to walnut-sized; tend to be wormier west of Cascades.

HABITAT - open woods and brushlands on both sides of the Cascades; found on the islands of Puget Sound; often near water, especially in eastern Washington.

EDIBILITY - excellent. Use the hips dried or fresh. For sweeter hips, harvest them soon after the first frost of the year. Rose hips are high in vitamin C. They are also a source of iron, calcium, and phosphorus. The seeds contain vitamin E. Use the dried and ground hips in soups, stews, teas, or make jams from the fresh fruit. Use the petals to liven-up a salad or jello. The petals also make a delicate jelly and have been used to make wine.

The generic name, *Rosa*, is the classical Latin name for the Rose.

drawing: top to bottom, Spring, Fall; ¾ x

Wild Strawberry

Wild Strawberry
Fragaria species
Rose Family - Roasaceae

There are 3 species of Strawberries in the Northwest. They look much the same, differing slightly in leaf size, color, hairiness, texture, and plant size. All of them are edible.

FORM - low herbaceous perennial with runners that root to form other plants; looks unmistakably like the horticultural type.

LEAVES - mostly basal; trifoliate or palmately compound with 3 leaflets; coursely toothed; hairy beneath and in some species above.

FLOWER - white flowers with yellow centers; 5 petals; a few flowers in a loose terminal cluster; April-June.

FRUIT - red; looks like the typical fruit, only pea-sized; very flavorful; late summer.

HABITAT - open wood to field; well drained soils; sea-level to 4,000 feet.

EDIBILITY - excellent. The berry is exquisite raw or cooked. The fruit is richer in flavor than store bought types. The strawberry is high in vitamins A and C, while the leaves are high in vitamin C. Leaves make a delicate tea, either fresh or dried. The fruit is high in calories, especially compared to most food that one can gather in the wild. Consider this one of the plants to know.

The ancient Latin name for the strawberry is 'fraga', hence the generic name of *Fragaria*.

drawing: left to right, Summer, Spring; 1x

Winter Cress

Winter Cress
Barbarea orthoceras Ledeb.
Mustard Family - Cruciferae

The time to be most familiar with Winter Cress is in the late winter, January-March. It survives well in mild climates, such as those in the Puget Sound region.

FORM - herb; rosette of dark green, shiny leaves during the winter months of Jan.-March; 10-20 inches tall stem with a taproot after the first year; biennial or perennial.

leaves - basal leaves 2-5 inches long; 2-10, deeply cleft, lateral lobes on the leaves with roundish terminal lobe (the largest); stem leaves either similar to basal leaves (reduced in size), or simple; leaf tastes peppery and spicy.

FLOWER - yellow flowers on a tall stem; the minute blooms ascending the stem, at the stem base seed pods will be forming while at the top buds will not yet have flowered; April-June.

FRUIT - seed, in a 1-2 inch long slender capsule; more peppery tasting when green than the leaves.

HABITAT - wet places; rich soils; meadows, streambanks, and moist woods; native of Eurasia.

EDIBILITY - excellent. The fresh leaves add zest to salads and sandwiches. They are also quite tasty cooked. In the early spring the roots have a hot peppery taste, much like horseradish.

Barbarea is in honor of St. Barbara of the fourth century.

drawing: left to right, Winter, Spring, Fall; ¼x

Wood Sorrel

Wood Sorrel
Oxalis oregana Nutt.
Buckwheat Family - Polygonaceae

FORM - low perennial herb averaging 8 inches tall; many plants in large patches forming smooth carpets.

LEAVES - 3 leaflets, looking like the leaves of clover; long leaf stems; leaflets 1-2 inches broad; leaves close up in darkness, in the rain, and with lack of water.

FLOWER - white with purple veins; solitary; 5 petals; 1-2 inches across; April-June.

HABITAT - deep woods; shade and moisture; sea-level to 4,000 feet; common along the coastal region; rare east of the Cascades.

EDIBILITY - excellent. Eat any part of this plant in small quantities only because of the high concentration of oxalic acid, which causes the pleasantly bitter taste. Use the leaves and stems fresh as a salad vegetable or cooked, especially with another green that needs a flavor addition, such as Nettle.

Oxalis comes from the Greek word, 'oxys', meaning sharp, because of the taste of the oxalic acid in the plant. *Oregana* means Oregon, where the plant grows in great numbers, especially along the coast.

drawing: Spring; 1x

Yarrow
Achillea millefolium L.
Composite Family - Compositae

FORM - herb with branched stems; rosette of fern-like leaves in the spring; 1-3 feet erect at maturity; dies back each winter.

LEAVES - fern-like; basal leaves are lance-shaped and divided many times; stem leaves are similar but much smaller in size.

FLOWER - flat-topped cluster of white flowers; generally spring blooming but can be found year round.

HABITAT - widespread; full sun; well drained soils; fields, vacant lots, pastures, roadways; great fields east of the Cascades; sea-level to middle elevations.

EDIBILITY - good. Use the dried leaves, flowers, or seeds for a tea. The leaves can be gathered any time that they are green, while the flowers are harvested in the spring and summer and the seeds are picked in the fall.

   Achillea is in honor of the Greek hero Achilles. It is said that he used this herb to aid his ailing soldiers, perhaps as a poultice or as a hot beverage. *Millefolium* refers to the many leaf divisions, giving the plant the fern-like appearance. The young plants in the spring particularly look like ferns.

drawing: Summer; ½x

Poisonous Plants

Baneberry

Baneberry
Actaea rubra (Ait.) Willd.
Buttercup Family - Ranunculaceae

FORM - perennial herb with 1 to several erect stems; 1-3 feet tall; leaf pattern very striking.

LEAVES - stem leaves only; large compound leaves; 1-4 inches long, lobed, and sharply toothed; leaflets egg-shaped in outline.

FLOWER - numerous, tiny, white flowers forming a dense cluster; 1-3 inch long cluster at top of stem; few clusters per plant; May-July.

FRUIT - red sometimes white; pea-sized; roundish; Aug.-Oct. *not edible.*

HABITAT - moist well drained soils; partial shade; grows inconspicuously in other low growing greenery; along streambanks, moist rock slopes, seasonal seepage areas; seldom more than a few growing together; sea-level to subalpine regions.

POISONOUS - Eating the fruit of the Europeon Baneberry has caused death according to the literature. The responsible toxin is thought to be ranunculin, which acts as a severe gastrointestinal irritant. Although there is no reported loss of life due to the Baneberry in our area, one is safest to consider the entire plant as highly poisonous.

There is a Baneberry, *Actaea alba*, which has white fruit. It is less common than the infrequently found red Baneberry and is just as poisonous.

The generic name, *Actaea*, is from the early Greek word 'aktea', for the elder tree. The resemblance of Baneberry to the elder tree is probably through the leaves. *Rubra* means red and *alba* means white, both are descriptive of the fruit color.

drawing: Summer - Fall; ¼x

Bittersweet Nightshade

Bittersweet Nightshade (Woody Nightshade)
Solanum dulcamara L.
Nightshade Family - Solanaceae

FORM - perennial with woody lower stems and herbaceous upper stems; 2-10 feet long trailing or climbing stems.

LEAVES - alternately arranged; 1-3 inches long with 2 lobes or leaflets near the base (some leaves lack the leaflets); broadly egg-shaped.

FLOWER - purple reflexed petals with a protruding yellow center; showy; 10-25 flowers in an open cluster; flowers are ½ inch long; May-Aug.

FRUIT - glossy, juicy fruit; green when immature and red at maturity; pea-sized; Aug.-Oct. *not edible.*

HABITAT - rich, moist soils; full to partial sun; associated with thickets and low brush; sea-level to 1,000 feet; native to Eurasia, now well established in the United States and southern Canada.

POISONOUS - All parts contain the toxin solanine, with the attractive red fruit containing the least quantity. Solanine first causes irritation and injury to the digestive tract, and then, after being absorbed through the injured tissue into the blood stream, causes malfunctions in the nervous system. Symptoms of poisoning are nervousness, abdominal pain, vomiting, diarrhea, shock and depression. Although poisonous, Bittersweet Nightshade is seldom eaten in a large enough quantity to be fatal.

drawing: Summer - Fall; ¼x

Buttercup

Buttercup (Crowfoot)
Ranunculus species
Buttercup Family - Ranunculaceae

FORM - ½-2 feet tall, generally perennial herbs; often with hairs; inconspicuous plants except when flowering; one of the first yellow flowering plants to show color in the early spring.

LEAVES - generally both basal and stem leaves; deeply lobed and-or compound leaves; 1-3 inch long leaf blades; frequently long leaf stems.

FLOWER - yellow; showy; fine, shiny petals; ½-1 inch flowers at the top of the flower stalk.

HABITAT - moist or wet soils; full sun to partial shade; pastures, fields, meadows; sea-level to alpine; large fields in the rural areas of the Puget Sound region are yellow colored in May due to this plant.

POISONOUS - Buttercups contain the toxin ranunculin, which acts as a severe gastrointestinal irritant. Although some Buttercups contain less toxins than others, all should be considered poisonous. Livestock rarely feed on the plant, perhaps due to its bitter taste.

   Ranunculus comes from the Latin 'rana' meaning frog. The reference is to the aquatic habitat of some species. The common name Crowfoot refers to the shape of the leaf in some species.
   Buttercups are easily confused with the Large Leaf Avens and cinquefoils. All are yellow, but only the Buttercups have shiny petals.

drawing: Late Spring - Summer; 1x

Death Camas

Death Camas
Zigadenus paniculatus (Nutt.) Wats.
Lily Family - Liliaceae

FORM - perennial herb with an elongated onion-like bulb; long, grass-like leaves arising from a clump; inconspicuous plant when not in flower.

LEAVES - mostly basal; 6-12 inches long; narrow and grass-like; leaves not hollow.

FLOWER - elongated cluster of many, off-white flowers; 6 look alike petals and sepals with a partly heart-shaped gland at the base of each; individual flowers average ⅛ inch across; ½-1½ foot tall flower stem; April-June.

HABITAT - open, dry locales; sagebrush desert, open Lodgepole or Ponderosa Pine forest; often grows in fields of the edible Camas; primarily east of the Cascades; sea-level to 2,000 feet.

POISONOUS - Death Camas contains poisonous alkaloids, which are similar to those in False Hellebore. The toxins act through the nervous system. Some symtoms of poisoning are increased salivation, digestive upset, abdominal pain, vomiting and diarrhea. There are several species of Death Camas; all are poisonous, although they differ in amount of toxin. As little as 6 pounds of one species of Death Camas eaten by a 100 pound sheep is a lethal dosage. In some states these spring plants cause the greatest loss of life in sheep of any plant. To man the greatest danger seems to be in the mistaken identity of this plant with the edible, blue-flowering Camas. The confusion occurs in the early spring or fall when neither of the plants is blooming. Another case when mistaken identity is apt to happen is in gathering Wild Onions. If the plant smells like an onion, then it is an onion, and if it doesn't, it isn't!

    Zigadenus is from the Greek words 'zugon', meaning yoke, and 'aden', meaning gland, referring to the glands circling the flower center. *Paniculatus* refers to the shape of the flower cluster on this particular plant. Death Camas received its name because the plant appears like the Camas, which has much established Indian tradition and use behind it. Camas is the Indian name for the edible bulb.
    Mountain Death Camas, *Zigadenus elegans* Pursh, is different mainly in two ways. Individual flowers average ¼ inch across and the habitat is above 2,500 feet and can be found on the west side of the Cascades.

drawing: Spring; ¾x

False Hellebore

False Hellebore
Veratrum californicum Durand.
Lily Family - Liliaceae

FORM - stout and striking perennial herb, 3-6 feet tall; many broad, coarsely veined leaves; thick rootstock.

LEAVES - many alternately arranged leaves; oval and 6-15 inches long; clasping the stem; reduced in size and more narrow ascending the stem; each leaf folded lengthwise like the pleats in a skirt, most distinctive.

FLOWER - white or greenish-white; dense clusters of small flowers cover the upper 1-3 of the stalk; June-Aug.

HABITAT - open swamps, meadows, and creek bottoms; lowlands to 7,000 feet; one of the primary plants that cover subalpine fields in the Cascades.

POISONOUS - The several alkaloids act on the nervous system in such a way as to cause the small arteries of the body to expand in diameter and the small veins to contract. They also slow the rate and force of the heart's contraction. The over-all result is reduced blood pressure. The purified alkaloids from False Hellebore are sometimes used in medicine to produce this effect. False Hellebore poisoning is rare, because the plant is rarely eaten in sufficient quantity by man or animal. The particular danger of this plant is when the young plant is mistaken for Skunk Cabbage, which some persons consider edible after cooking.

Veratrum comes from the Latin word 'vere', meaning true, and 'ater', meaning black, referring to the black roots of this plant. The specific name, *californicum*, refers to the state where the plant was first collected and described in the literature in 1855.

drawing: Summer; ⅛x

Foxglove
Digitalis purpurea L.
Figwort Family - Scrophulariaceae

One would not ordinarilly eat this plant, however it could be mistaken by a novice for a young Burdock, or, less likely, Curly Dock. All these have adequate distinguishing features so the confusion is unnecessary.

FORM - stout perennial; the first year a rosette of large, soft leaves and the second year a 2-5 feet tall stem with flowers on the upper half.

LEAVES - basal leaves 4-12 inches long, fuzzy, and widely lance-shaped; the stem leaves similar but reduced in size ascending the stem.

FLOWER - white, pink-purple and spotted; showy; 1-2 inches long with a tubular shape; flowers grow ¾ of the way around the stalk and on the upper half; June-July.

HABITAT - shady, well drained soils; mostly disturbed sites; generally full sun; along roadsides and logged-off areas; sea-level to 2,500 feet; found primarily west of the Cascades; native of Europe, now naturalized here.

POISONOUS - All parts contain the toxin digitalis, a drug used for particular heart conditions. A minute quantity beneficially paralyzes some heart muscles, while a slightly larger dosage can fatally paralyze the heart. Symptoms of poisoning are nausea, diarrhea, stomach aches, headache, irregular pulse, tremors and convulsions.

Digitalis is a Latin word pertaining to an indicidual flower looking like a finger. The specific name, *purpurea*, refers to the common purple color phase of the flower.

drawing: top to bottom, 2nd year Summer; ⅛x
1st year Summer; ¼x

Larkspur
Delphinium species
Buttercup Family - Ranunculaceae

There are more than a dozen species of Larkspur in the Northwest. They may be divided into 2 groups, the 3-6 foot tall Larkspurs and those that grow to less than 3 feet tall. The taller ones inhabit mountainous elevations and die back in the fall. The short Larkspurs thrive in lower elevations and die back in late summer.

FORM - erect perennial herbs, 2-6 feet tall; finely divided leaves.

LEAVES - basal or alternate on the stem; simple leaves but palmately lobed to deeply divided into 3-5 divisions; primary divisions redivided; obvious leaf stalks.

FLOWER - bluish to purple sometimes whitish; showy; irregularly shaped flower; 1 backwards projecting spur; few to several flowers on an erect stem; April-July.

HABITAT - dry to moist locales; full sun to partial shade; sagebrush lands, Ponderosa or Lodgepole Pine forests, scree slopes, meadows; sea-level to alpine regions.

POISONOUS - The many Larkspurs should be considered poisonous. They cause great loss of life in cattle on the western range lands. Sheep are unaffected under ordinary range conditions. Experiments indicate that the foliage is highly poisonous in the spring and becomes decreasingly toxic with maturity. The seeds, too, contain a high concentration of poison. The toxin effects the nervous system. The effects on man are not well established.

Delphinium is the Latinized form of the Greek word for these plants, 'Delphinion'. To the imagination of an ancient Greek the nectary of the Larkspur had the shape of a dolphin, hence the name.

drawing: Spring - Summer; ¾x

Lupine

Lupine (Bluebonnet)
Lupinus species
Pea Family - Leguminosae

FORM - 1-2½ feet tall, bushy, perennial herbs; non-woody stems.

LEAVES - alternate on the stem; palmately compound; long leaf stalk; 5-17 leaflets; leaflets are 1-3 inches long and lance-shaped.

FLOWER - light blue to blue-purple and yellow; showy; many, butterfly-like flowers in a linear cluster; ½-1 inch long flowers; April-July.

FRUIT - greenish; pea pod type; 1-3 inches long; hairy; June-Sept.; *not edible.*

HABITAT - widespread; sandy soils full sun; sagebrush deserts, conifer forests, mountain meadows; sea-level to 5,000 feet.

POISONOUS - The more than dozen different species of Lupines in the Northwest are difficult to distinguish from one another. Although some plants are toxic and others are not, the entire genus should be avoided. Seeds and mature plants contain the most poison. Even drying does not eliminate or reduce the toxin. Sheep are the most commonly affected under normal range conditions. Symptoms of poisoning are heavy breathing, trembling, and convulsions. The greatest danger of this plant is when someone mistakenly decides that because the fruit looks like the edible garden pea, then it too must be edible.

Lupinus comes from the Latin word 'lupus' meaning wolf. Since Lupines grow in poor or sandy media, it was thought that they robbed the soil of minerals. Wolves, too, were thought to be troublesome robbers, so the plant received its name. However, Lupines actually enrich the soil. Nitrogen-fixing bacteria associated with the roots take elemental nitrogen from the atmosphere and change it into a nitrogen compound suitable for plant use. We are finding out more about wolves, too.

drawing: Spring - Summer; ¼ x

Poison Hemlock

Poison Hemlock
Conium maculatum L.
Parsley Family - Umbelliferae

Because Poison Hemlock is one of the most deadly plants in the Pacific Northwest and because it is widespread, it is important that every forager be aware of its presence and make efforts to be able to recognize it. Here are some features that will help. The plants grow in groups with the foliage of the young ones looking like that of ferns. This fern-like appearance is another danger of Poison Hemlock, especially for persons who might act upon the belief that all ferns are edible. The plant is about 3 feet tall before it produces a cluster of white flowers. By this time many purple splotches are evident on the stem.

Water Hemlock, *Cicuta* species, and Poison Hemlock are sometimes confused with one another. Both belong to the Parsley family and each shares features that are displayed by the other. However, once one becomes familiar with Poison Hemlock, it is easy to distinguish it from the deadly poisonous Water Hemlock.

FORM - 2-10 feet tall, freely branched biennial; purple spots or mottling on the stem; stem hollow; stout, carrot-like taproot; unique odor.

LEAVES - fern-like leaves; pinnately compound; blades of larger leaves commonly 5-10 inches long.

FLOWER - many small white flowers in a flat-topped cluster that is 1-4 inches across; many clusters per plant; May-July.

FRUIT - ⅛ inch long with ribs; looks nearly identical to anise seeds; July-Sept.; *Highly poisonous.*

HABITAT - moist, disturbed soils; full sun; low elevations; native to Eurasia, now well established over most of North America.

HIGHLY POISONOUS - All parts are poisonous, especially the seeds. The toxic alkaloids work by depressing the function of the central nervous system. Death occurs when the muscles used for breathing become paralyzed. Symptoms are gastrointestinal dysfunction and pain, death of some tissue, muscular weakness respiratory paralysis and convulsions. One of the reasons why this plant is so often fatal is because there is no known antidote. From the symptoms of dying, it is apparent that Poison Hemlock was used to prepare a concoction which the Greek philosopher Socrates drank.

Conium is derived from the ancient Greek word, 'koneion', their name for this plant. *Maculatum* means spotted in reference to the characteristic purple spots on the stems, especially on the older plants.

drawing: Summer; ⅛x

Red Elderberry

Red Elderberry
Sambucus racemosa L.
Honeysuckly Family - Caprifoliaceae

The fruit of the plant is eaten by birds, especially robins and band-tailed pigeons. For those persons interested in attracting birds to their garden and home this is a choice shrub to plant. It is a native plant and is therefore adapted to the soils and climate of western Washington, requiring little gardening attention.

FORM - shrub with several pithy stems; 6-20 feet tall; sometimes a single trunk rather than several stems.

LEAVES - 5-9 leaflets with each leaflet lance-shaped and 2-4 inches long; leaves are opposite on the stem.

FLOWER - whitish; 6-12 inch tall pyramidal cluster, often drooping; bright red with no waxy coating; May-July.

HABITAT - open fields to dense underbrush; conifer or alder forests and roadsides; lowlands to 4,000 feet; abundant west of the Cascades.

REPORTEDLY POISONOUS - The fruit could possibly be used cooked, as in jams or jellies. I have eaten some of the fresh fruit and found them not at all pleasing. I have sampled 2 different jellies made from the cooked fruit and found them having an almost pleasant taste. With a little work, it might make an OK jelly. At the very best this is a marginal food source. One would not be making any mistakes to leave the fruit to the birds. The leaves and twigs should *not* be eaten.

Sambucus is the classical name for this plant. *Racemosa* refers to the particular type of flower cluster.

drawing: top to bottom, Spring; ¼x
Summer; ¼x

Swamp Laurel

Swamp Laurel
Kalmia polifolia Wang.
Heather Family - Ericaceae

The strongly inrolled edges function to minimize water loss through evaporation. Even in a swamp, water for plant usage is unavailable when it is frozen, which is most of the year at high elevations.

Within the pink bowl of the flower lie 10 stamens. Each rests in a depression in the crinkled corolla. When the pollen is ripe, a nectar seeking insect triggers any number of stamens. The mature stamen catapults from the pouch and deposits the viable grains on the insect. The insect becomes the vehicle of pollination, accomplished when the male germ is deposited on the female part of another Swamp Laurel flower. One may easily take part in this drama with a small piece of grass and a ripe flower.

FORM - woody, perennial, shrub; evergreen; ½-1½ feet tall; trailing branches.

LEAVES - crowded; oblong; ½-1½ inches long; nearly no leaf stalk; evergreen; leathery; grayish beneath; margins generally inrolled.

FLOWER - deep pink to rose; showy; clustered at stem tips; saucer-shaped; ½ inch across; anther pouches in the 10 petals and sepals; June-Sept.

HABITAT - wet, acidic soils; full sun; bogs, seepage areas, swamps; 2,000 feet to alpine regions.

POISONOUS - Swamp Laurel contains the poisonous compound andromedotoxin, a resinoid carbohydrate. Symptoms of poisoning, which are increased salivation, nausea, vomiting, and severe abdominal pain, usually appear within 6 hours after eating. A small quantity of leaves is enough to cause symptoms. The Delaware Indians reportedly used a species of laurel for suicide. There is also conflicting data on poisoning by laurel honey.

Kalmia is in honor of Peter Kalm, an early botanist and student of Carl Linnaeus. Linnaeus is the man who initiated the system of naming and classifying plants for modern science. *Polifolia* means whitened leaves.

drawing: Summer; 3x

Water Hemlock

Water Hemlock
Cicuta douglasii (DC.) Coult. & Rose.
Parsley Family - Umbelliferae

FORM - a stout perennial with 1 or a few erect stems, 2-5 feet tall; 1-5 tuberous rootstocks that are 1-3 inches long and ½ inch wide; rootstock shows horizontal chambers when cut vertically; the cut stalk exudes a yellow, oily liquid; the oil is especially poisonous.

LEAVES - the basal and stem leaves are similar in size and shape; stem leaves alternate in arrangement along the stem; 1-3 times divided in a pinnate way; well defined, lance-shaped, 2-4 inch long leaflets; leaflets have toothed margins with primary lateral veins striking the "valleys", not the "hills"

FLOWER - small, white flowers grow in a flat-topped cluster, 2-5 inches across; June-Aug.

FRUIT - 2-sectioned, fruit pod with corky ribs; ⅛ inch long Aug.-Oct.

HABITAT - marshes, edges of streams, and ditches from lowlands to 2,000 feet.

HIGHLY POISONOUS - Water Hemlock is one of the *most poisonous* plants in the Northwest. All of it is fatally poisonous with the roots being the most toxic. Reportedly, the basal part from one plant contains enough toxin to be fatal to a cow. The plant causes death to spring feeding cattle. At this time the animals are hungry for fresh greens and Water Hemlock sometimes provides the deadly foliage.

Cicuta is the classical Latin name and *douglasii* is in honor of the botanist David Douglass, who explored the flora of the Pacific Northwest more than a century ago.

drawing: Summer; ½x

Western Bleeding Heart

Western Bleeding Heart
Dicentra formosa (Andr.) Walpers.
Fumitory Family - Fumariaceae

FORM - 1-2 feet tall, perennial herb; shade-loving, early flowering plant; feathery leaves.

LEAVES - basal leaves; 3-4 times compound; leaflets average 1 inch long; 5-15 inch long leaf stalk.

FLOWER - pink to purple and showy; 1 inch long; bi-symmetrical flower; up to 12 flowers per stem; April-June.

FRUIT - young green "pods" protrude through the spent flower; 1-2 inches long; May-July; *not edible.*

HABITAT - moist, shady locales; streambanks, conifer forests; sea-level to mid elevations; abundant west of the Cascades; numerous plants grow together.

POISONOUS - Bleeding Heart contains the toxin alkaloid isoquinoline. Cattle have died from consuming *Dicentra*. Little is known about its specific effects. Perhaps the only reason why anyone would try this plant is because the fruit has a similar appearance to that of the garden pea.

Dicentra comes from the Greek words 'dis', meaning twice and 'kentron', meaning spur and referring to the spurs of the flower. *Formosa* is Latin and means graceful or beautiful.

drawing: Spring; ¾x

Wild Cucumber

Wild Cucumber
Marah oreganus (T. & G.) Howell.
Gourd Family - Cucurbitaceae

FORM - stout perennial with a much enlarged, woody root; 8-30 feet long trailing or climbing stems; tendrils, like those of grapes, used for climbing.

LEAVES - alternately arranged; nearly 6 inches long; lobed; heart-shaped at the base.

FLOWER - white, bell-shaped, and 5-lobed; several male flowers on a foot long stem with the female flower being solitary; both are auxiliary; May-June.

FRUIT - greenish; egg-shaped; 2-3 inches long; weakly spined or almost smooth; 1-2 seeds in each of 2-4 cavities; Aug.-Oct.; *not edible.*

HABITAT - rich, moist soil; full to partial sun; sea-level to 1,000 feet; mostly west of the Cascades.

POSSIBLY POISONOUS - Leslie Haskin writes that the seeds "are probably poisonous to human beings. Certain Indians are said to have used the seeds of similar species as a means of committing suicide."

Marah comes from the Hebrew word 'marah' meaning bitter, in allusion to the intensely bitter root. *Oreganus* means Oregon.

drawing: Summer; ¼x

Recipes

The intent with these recipes is to share personal plant cooking experiences with the reader. Besides being a follow-up to the section entitled "Edibility", this is an effort to satisfy those persons who enjoy cooking from recipes. These recipes have a further advantage to those for whom this type of cooking is a new adventure. Here are opportunities to use recipes and learn from other person's experiences. Unless otherwise indicated the recipes were originated by the author.

Soups

Hiker's Consumme (Sheep Sorrel Consumme) (Tamara & Doug)

3 cups water
3 teaspoons or 3 cubes chicken bouillon
6 dried Wild Onion bulbs (perhaps more bulbs if using fresh Wild Onions)
2 Tablespoons butter
¼ teaspoon salt
⅛ teaspoon pepper
1 teaspoon dried parsley leaves
a pinch dried Water Cress leaves
¼ cup chopped, fresh Sheep Sorrel leaves

optional: 1 cup broken spaghetti noodles

Mix all ingredients except the Sheep Sorrel in warming water. When the ingredients have blended well together, a minimum of 10 minutes, put the Sheep Sorrel in the pot for the last 5 minute simmer. Serve the consumme, with a salty cracker, to your hiking companion.

Chickweed Soup (Tamara)

4-5 cups chopped Chickweed leaves & stems
4-5 cups water
1 teaspoon onion salt
1 teaspoon celery salt
(2-3 teaspoons plain salt as a substitute for the above salts)
½ teaspoon lemon pepper or black pepper
2 small diced potatoes
1 sliced carrot
¼ cup chopped onion
1 cup chopped celery
add ½ cup chopped Sheep Sorrel leaves & stems if available and desired

Bring to a boil, then cook over low heat for at least 1 hour. For heartier soup, add 1-2 cups milk and 1 Tablespoon butter.

Makes 4-8 servings.

Curly Dock Soup. (Johanna)

2 Tablespoons oil
½ cup chopped mushrooms
1 chopped onion
¼ cup wheat germ
1 sliced carrot
5 cups water
3 Tablespoons tamari or soy sauce
1 chopped and seeded tomato
1-2 cups young Curly Dock leaves
1 stalk celery & leaves

Brown mushrooms and onion in oil. Add wheat germ and sliced carrot.
Heat. Add water, tamari and tomato. Cover. Bring to a slow boil, then turn
off heat. Add chopped greens and celery. Cover tightly. Serve in 5 minutes.

Makes 4-6 servings.

Early Summer Hearty Soup

½ - ¾ lbs. cooked & chopped turkey
1 cup turkey broth
1 cup of juice from cooked pinto or kidney beans
3 cups water
1 cup chopped Mustard leaves & flower buds
2 cups chopped Water Cress leaves & stems
One-third cup chopped Sheep Sorrel leaves & stems
1 cup noodles
4-5 dozen dried Mustard seed capsules
¼ teaspoon celery seeds
½ teaspoon onion salt
½ teaspoon salt
¼ teaspoon basil
1 Tablespoon dried parsley leaves

Simmer the turkey, spices, and chopped onion in the broth, bean juice, and
water for 2-3 hours. Add the chopped greens of Water Cress and Mustard
and continue to simmer for another half hour. Add the leaves and stems of
Sheep Sorrel and the noodles at the same time and cook the soup until the
noodles are done.

Makes 6-8 servings.

Cattail Consumme

3 cups water
½ cup chopped inner leaves of Cattail
¼ cup finely chopped onion
2 cubes chicken or beef bouillon
1 Tablespoon butter
¼ teaspoon salt
⅛ teaspoon pepper or lemon pepper
a pinch of dried Water Cress leaves

Add all ingredients to the water and simmer, after coming to a boil, for a couple of hours. This is a light soup to be served at the beginning of a long, pleasurable meal.

Cooked Greens And The Like

Chickweed and Eggs in Mornay Sauce (Tamara)

4 cups chopped Chickweed leaves & stems
1 Tablespoon chopped Sheep Sorrel
2 teaspoons chopped yellow or white onion
2 teaspoons chopped celery
6 poached or soft boiled eggs
One-third cup butter
1 teaspoon salt
⅛ teaspoon cayenne
2 cups milk
1 cup cheddar cheese (grated)
¼ cup parmesan cheese

Cook vegies 'til just tender, taking care not to overcook. Put vegies in bottom of 1½ quart casserole. Place eggs on vegies. In a sauce pan melt butter and blend in flour and seasonings. Add cheddar cheese. Gradually add milk and cook, stirring constantly 'til sauce is thick and smooth and cheese is melted completely. Pour sauce over Chickweed and eggs. Sprinkle parmesan cheese on top. Put under broiler 'til lightly browned.

Makes 4-6 servings.

Flower Buds and Cheese

Bring to a boil 1½ cups of salt water. Add 2 cups of flowers and flower buds of Lamb's Quarters (the top 2-6 inches of the plant which can be gathered from June to August). Add a tablespoon of fresh lemon and a couple tablespoons of butter and cook for 7-10 minutes. Serve in a bowl with a slab of butter and grated sharp cheddar cheese. Add some of the juice, for it helps keep the greens hot and is extremely tasty and nutritious.

Lamb's Quarters and Cattail

Bring 1 cup of salted water to a boil. Cut into 1 inch sections 2 male flower stems of the Cattail. Add this along with the cut-up lower-inner tender leaves from 3 Cattail stalks. Add 1 cup of young shoots and leaves of Lamb's Quarters. A teaspoon of butter, salt, and ½ teaspoon of fresh lemon impart a pleasing flavor. Cook the preparation for 5-10 minutes. Serves 2.

The male flower stems are prime only in June and July at sea-level.

Fritter Batter (Johanna)

1½ cups unbleached flour
2 eggs
1 Tablespoon oil
1 teaspoon salt
1 Tablespoon parsley
1 cup stale beer or white wine

Mix until smooth. Refrigerate until wanted. Dip dry vegetables into batter and deep fry. Drain on brown bags.
Vegies for fritters:

Purslane stems
Dandelion flowers (unopened)
Fern fiddleheads
Wild Onions
Cattail inner leaves

Give your imagination free rein and try some other wild vegies. Eat while WARM.

Cornish Game Hen & Blue Elderberry Stuffing

3 Tablespoons dried Blue Elderberry fruit

1 cup partially cooked brown rice	¼ cup chopped celery
3 Tablespoons wheat germ	¼ cup chopped walnuts
½ cup chopped onion	1 Tablespoon dried parsley leaves
small handful of mung sprouts	¼ teaspoon pepper
1 egg	½ teaspoon salt
¼ cup raisins	¼ cup white wine.

Blend all ingredients together and stuff. This is enough stuffing to do a small chicken.

Breads

Chickweed Bread (Tamara)

2 cups chopped Chickweed leaves & stems
¼ cup minced white or yellow onion
6 Tablespoons margarine
3 cups flour
1 teaspoon salt
¾ cup warm water
1 package yeast

Saute onion and Chickweed in 2 tablespoons of margarine 'til tender, not brown. Dissolve salt in water. Melt rest of margarine. Combine with water and Chickweed. Mix yeast with flour. Slowly add Chickweed mixture to flour, working 'til no longer sticks to fingers. Form into a ball. Let stand ½ hour. Bake at 400 degrees for 35-40 minutes.

Nettle Herb Bread (Tamara)

1 package dry yeast
¼ cup warm water
¾ cup scalded milk
2 Tablespoons sugar
1½ teaspoon salt
2 Tablespoon margarine
1 beaten egg
3 Tablespoons dried and finely ground Nettle leaves
2 teaspoons celery seed
3 cups flour

Dissolve yeast in water. Combine milk with sugar, salt, and margarine. Cool to lukewarm. Add yeast. Add egg, Nettle, celery seed. Stir in 2 cups flour and beat dough 'til smooth. Gradually stir in flour to make workable dough. Knead. Place in greased bowl. Turn so oiled on all sides. Let rise, about 1½ hours. Punch down and leave for 15 minutes. Shape dough into a round loaf. Place in a greased 8" pie pan. Let rise 'til doubled. Bake 35-40 minutes at 400 degrees.

Mother French's Biscuits (Tamara)

2 cups flour
4 teaspoons baking powder.
½ teaspoon salt
¾ cup mulk
¼ cup lard

Mix together the dry ingredients, then cut in the shortening. Add milk all at once and stir quickly. Do not knead dough. Shape biscuits. Makes 8 2-inch biscuits 1 inch thick. Bake 10-15 minutes at 400 degrees.

This is a recipe to which one could add ¼ cup dried Pineapple Weed flower heads, or ¼ cup dried and finely ground Rose hips, or 2 Tablespoons of dried and finely ground Nettle leaves, or 2 Tablespoons of dried Chickweed leaves & stems. Pineapple Weed and Rose hipe are the most tasty.

Jams, Jellies, And Sauces

Rose Hip Sauce with Honey (Tamara & Doug)

2½ cups water
4 cups washed rose hips
5 medium apples (peeled & cored)
1 cup honey

Slice apples and peel if desired. Add to water and cook over medium heat to apple sauce consistency. Blend hips at low speed in electric osterizer until smooth. It may be necessary to add the hips a few at a time, depending upon the type of osterizer. Add the apple sauce to osterizer and mix both fruits at medium speed until uniform mixture. Add the honey and continue to blend until smooth. If the seeds in the hips are distasteful, one can remove them by straining the mixture through cheese cloth. Makes 4-5 cups, more than enough for immediate use. Give some away to a fellow forager or surprise a friend with a gift.

Apple-Mint Jelly (Johanna)

4 cups apple juice
3 cups sugar
1 Tablespoon lemon concentrate
Fresh Mint leaves, crushed and tied in a bag

Wash and chop apples. Cover with water. Boil until soft and mash. Strain through 2 layers of cheese cloth. Simmer 4 cups of this apple juice. Add sugar and simmer until thickened. Add lemon. Dip bag of mint into the pan of warm jelly until the taste and flavor is right.

Blackberry-Apple Jam (Johanna)

4 cups mashed Blackberries (all types are good)
2 cups apple juice (refer to Apple-Mint Jelly)
5 cups sugar

Simmer berries and juice 5 minutes. Strain this mixture through a sieve.
Add sugar. Simmer until thickened.

Apple-Salal Sauce (Johanna)

4 cups cored apples
1 cup water
2 Tablespoons molasses
½-1 cup Salal berries (or any seasonal berry)

Wash and core apples; cook (in covered stainless pot) with water &
molasses until soft. Remove from heat. Mash. Add berries. Cover. Serve
in ½ hour.

Red Huckleberry-Apple Jam (Tamara & Doug)

2 cups Red Huckleberries
2 large apples (peeled & cored)
1½ cups water
¾ cups honey

Take Red Huckleberries, apple slices, water and bring to a boil, then reduce
heat to medium. Add the honey and stir. After the apples are crushed and
the mixture is smooth, take the pan off the burner and put the jam into jars.
Takes 30-45 minutes.

Oregon Grape-Plum Jam

4-5 cups Oregon Grape
2 cups pitted plums
½ cup honey
1½ cups water
Follow the directions for Red Huckleberry-Apple Jam. Makes 3-4 cups.

Salal Glaze for Poultry (Tamara)

Heat together ½ cup Salal jam or jelly
1 rounded teaspoon honey
¼ cup of sweet wine

Baste foul with the glaze the last 45 minutes of cooking.

Salad Stuff

Early Spring Delight

You can make an early spring (April-May) salad from some of the most tasty and succulent native greens. Mix the leaves and stems of Siberian Miner's lettuce and Chickweed, one loose cup of each. Add 2 Tablespoons of diced leaves of Sheep Sorrel along with diced lower-inner stalks of Cattail. Add some onions for flavor and mix all the greens. Sprinkle 1 Tablespoon of wheat germ. Serve with your favorite dressing. Serves 2.

French Salad Dressing

¼ cup white wine
¼ cup fresh lemon juice
1¼ cups salad oil
2 teaspoons ground Rose hips
1 teaspoon dried Water Cress
¼ teaspoon pepper
½ teaspoon Mustard seeds
1 teaspoon paprika
½ teaspoon sugar
1 teaspoon dried parsley leaves
2 Tablespoons catsup
¼ cup diced, fresh Sheep Sorrel
4 crushed pea-sized Wild Onion bulbs

Add all ingredients to a quart jar and shake vigorously. Keeps well in the refrigerator. Makes 2 cups.

Cool Beverages

Blackberry - Mint Cooler (Rickie)

2 cups ripe Blackberries (Pacific Blackberries are most flavorful but Himalayan are most plentiful)
¼ cup honey
3 cups water
3 dozen fresh Mint leaves (½ the quantity if dried mint leaves are used)

Mix the berries and honey in a blender until the mixture is uniform. Steep chopped Mint leaves in boiled water for 5 minutes. Remove the Mint leaves and add the water to the berry syrup and blend for 1 minute. This makes about 6 cups of Blackberry-Mint Syrup, enough for 1 gallon (depending upon your taste) of cool drink when mixed with water, 7 Up, or tonic. If the berry seeds are a problem, remove them by squeezing the syrup through a nylon stocking.

A Revolutiona

12 oz. glass filled with ice cubes
½ shot lime
1 shot vodka
Fill the glass with Blackberry-Mint Syrup and stir
Twist of lime

A Red Ringer

12 oz. glass filled with ice cubes
½ shot of lime
1 shot of gin
Fill the glass with Blackberry-Mint syrup and stir
Twist of lime

Sheep Sorrel Cooler

5 cups water
¼ cup chopped, fresh Sheep Sorrel
3 pinches salt
2 teaspoons fresh lemon juice
4 Tablespoons sugar

Place all ingredients into a blender and blend on high for a couple of minutes. Strain and pour into a tall glass filled with ice cubes.

Green Czonker (Tamara)

12 oz. glass filled with ice cubes
1 shot vodka
Fill glass with Sheep Sorrel Syrup and stir
Twist of lime or lemon

Green Zinger

12 oz. glass filled with ice cubes
1 shot gin
Fill glass with Sheep Sorrel Syrup and stir
Twist of lime or lemon

Hot Beverages

These recipes all make 1 quart of hot beverage. Bring 1 quart of water to a boil, turn off heat and add the plant parts. Steep for 15-20 minutes. Adding honey tends to bring out the plant flavors as well as sweeten the drink. These "teas" are also good as iced beverages.

A hot beverage can be made from either fresh or dried plant parts. In either case, crushing the plant material just prior to steeping results in a more flavorful drink.

Blue Elderberry-Mint
1 Tablespoon ground Rose Hips
1 Tablespoon mashed, fresh Blue Elderberries
3-4 large Mint leaves
1 Tablespoon honey

Chokecherry-Mint
1 Tablespoon groond Rose Hips
2 Tablespoons mashed, fresh fruit of Chokecherry
3-4 Mint leaves
1 Tablespoon honey
Frozen Chokecherries that have been thawed can be used

Pineapple Weed
2 Tablespoons Pineapple Weed flower heads
1 Tablespoon Honey

Rose Hip
1½ Tablespoons ground Rose Hips
2 teaspoons honey
Adding a few dried Mint leaves makes a nice flavor change

Rose Hip-Pineapple Weed-Mint
A combination of the 3 best beverage plants
1 Tablespoon ground Rose Hips
1 Tablespoon Pineapple Weed flower heads
3-4 large Mint leaves
1 teaspoon honey

Dandelion Leaf-Sheep Sorrel
3 dozen Dandelion leaves
2 dozen Sheep Sorrel leaves
1 teaspoon honey
Heat together ½ cup Salal jam or jelly

Glossary

Many of the terms described here are pictured in the illustrated glossary which follows this one.

Alkaline - basic; opposite of acidic.

Alpine - above timberline; 5,000 to 7,000 feet in the Cascades.

Annual - a plant that goes through a complete life cycle in a single year.

Anther - the pollen containing part of the male portion of the flower.

Basal - from (at) the base of a plant.

Berry - a fruit that is uniformly pulpy or juicy.

Biennial - a plant that goes through a complete life cycle in two years.

Blade - the larger part of the leaf.

Blanch - to make white or pale by keeping out light to improve taste.

Bract - a modified leaf, usually near the base of a flower.

Bulb - an underground leaf bud with fleshy scales such as with an onion.

Calyx - the lower and generally least colorful part of a flower; a term that includes all the sepals.

Capsule - a dry, compound fruit that opens at maturity.

Compound - composed of more than 1 part, such as with some leaves.

Corm - a solid bulb, such as with **Claytonia lanceolata**.

Corolla - all the petals.

Diskflower - small tubular flowers that make-up the center part of the head of flowers of most Composite family members.

Disturbed soils - soils that have been affected by man, such as gardens, roadsides, and construction sites.

Ecology - the study of organisms as they relate to their environment.

Evergreen - holding green leaves throughout the year.

Exsert - protrude or thrust out as with the flower of Bittersweet Nightshade.

Fertilization - the union of the male and female germ cells; different than pollination.

Filament - the stalk of the stamen.

Fruit - the seed containing part of a plant.

Genus - plural genera; a grouping (of plants) comprised of closely related species.

Gland - a group of cells, generally of the secreting type; examples are the glands at the base of the Chokecherry leaf and the glands on the flower of **Zigadenus**.

Habitat - the growing environment.

Head - a dense cluster of stalkless flowers; examples are the flowers of Dandelion, Yarrow, and Thistle.

Herb - a plant with no woody parts above the ground.

Herbaceous - not being of a woody nature.

Herbage - green foliage and sometimes stems.

Humus - the organic part of the soil, such as decaying leaves, twigs, bark, and wood.

Internode - between the nodes.

Linear - very narrow.

Merous - a suffix meaning having parts.

Node - the place on the stem from where a leaf emerges.

Oblong - a shape where the length is 2-3 times the width with the sides nearly parallel.

Oval - egg-shaped.

Ovary - that part of the pistil in which seeds are produced.

Palmate - radiating out from a central point as with the hand; often referring to leaf lobes or leaflets.

Perennial - lasting from year to year.

Perianth - a collective term which includes the sepals and petals.

Petal - generally the colorful part of the flower.

Petiole - the leaf stalk.

Pinnate - arranged along the sides of a common axis; often referring to leaf lobes or leaflets.

Pistil - the female or see-bearing organ of the flower.

Pollen - the golden grains of the anther that contain the male sex cells.

Rayflower - small ray-shaped flowers that are on the edge of the head of flowers of most Composite family members.

Rhizome - an underground, creeping root-like stem.

Rosette - a cluster of leaves in a circular form, usually at the base of the plant; examples are the first year plant of Foxglove and Evening Primrose.

Scree - small broken stones at the foot of a steep slope.

Sepal - the lower and generally least colorful part of the flower.

Simple - an undivided leaf; opposed to compound.

Species - the basic unit of scientific classification; the terms are generally descriptive, such as "album", meaning white, and "edule", meaning edible.

Sub - less than; approaching; nearly.

Stamen - the male or pollen-bearing organ of the flower.

Stigma - that part of the pistil which receives the pollen.

Style - the stalk of the pistil.

Succulent - juicy; fleshy, soft and thickened in texture.

Talus - a slope of fragmented rocks.

Taproot - a stout, vertical root that continues the main axis of the plant; examples are Poison Hemlock, Burdock, and some Mustards.

Taxon - a grouping of plants; generally of species.

Terminal - growing at the end of a branch or stem.

Timberline - the region where the tree population stops; about 5,000 to 7,000 feet in the Cascades.

Flower Structure

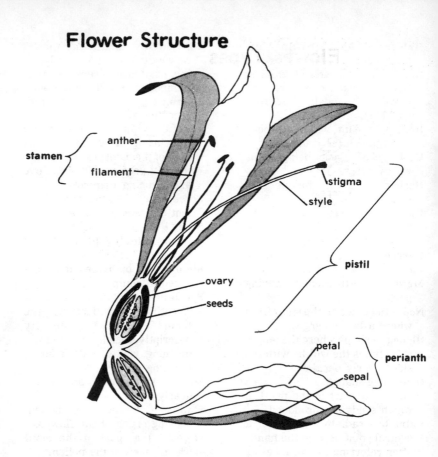

stamen { anther

filament

stigma

style

pistil

ovary

seeds

petal

sepal

perianth

Leaf Structure

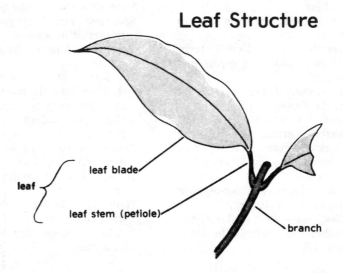

leaf { leaf blade

leaf stem (petiole)

branch

Flower Types

composite
(Dandelion)

pea-shaped
(Lupine)

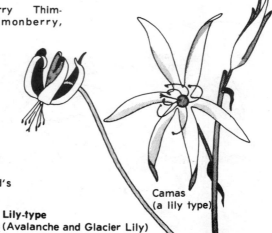

urn-shaped
(Blueberry Huckleberry,
Kinnikinnik)

Rose-type
(Rose, Strawberry Thim-
bleberry, Salmonberry,
Blackberry)

Mustard-type
(Winter Cress, Shepherd's
Purse, Mustard)

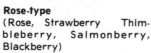

Lily-type
(Avalanche and Glacier Lily)

Camas
(a lily type)

Leaf Positions

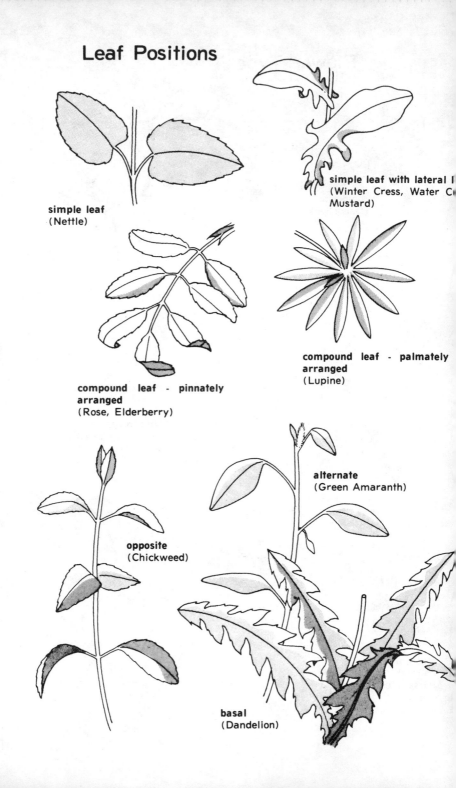

simple leaf
(Nettle)

simple leaf with lateral l
(Winter Cress, Water C
Mustard)

compound leaf - pinnately
arranged
(Rose, Elderberry)

compound leaf - palmately
arranged
(Lupine)

opposite
(Chickweed)

alternate
(Green Amaranth)

basal
(Dandelion)

Leaf Shapes

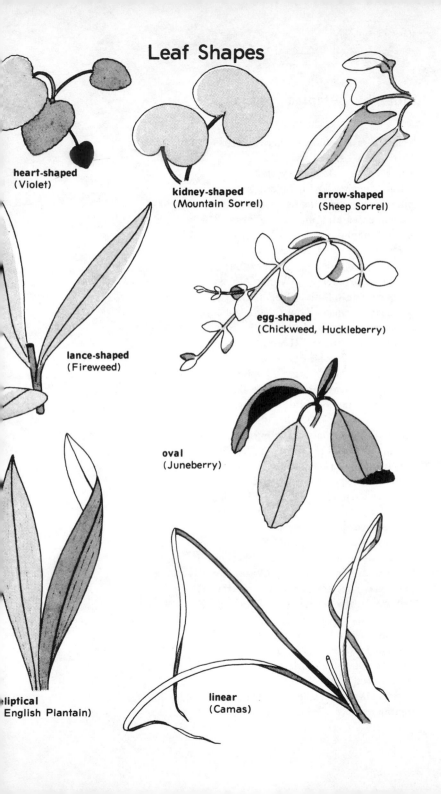

heart-shaped
(Violet)

kidney-shaped
(Mountain Sorrel)

arrow-shaped
(Sheep Sorrel)

lance-shaped
(Fireweed)

egg-shaped
(Chickweed, Huckleberry)

oval
(Juneberry)

elliptical
(English Plantain)

linear
(Camas)

Index by Botanical Name

Suggestions For Further Reading

Books about Edible Plants and Recipes

Berglund, Berndt and Clare C. Bolsby. **The Edible Wild**. New York: Charles Scribner's Sons, 1971.

Burt, Calvin P. and Frank G. Heyl. **Edible and Poisonous Plants of the Western States**. Lake Oswego, Oregon, 1970. (a deck of cards)

Gibbons, Euell. **Stalking the Healthful Herbs**. New York: David McKay Company, Inc., 1966.

Gibbons, Euell. **Stalking the Wild Asparagus**. New York: David McKay Company, Inc., 1962.

Identification Manuals

Clark, Lewis J. **Wild Flowers of British Columbia**. Sidney: Gray's Publishing Limited, 1973.

Fries, Mary A. **Wildflowers of Mount Rainier and the Cascades**. The Mount Rainier Natural History Association and The Mountaineers, 1970.

Haskins, Leslie L. **Wildflowers of the Pacific Coast**. Binfords & Mort, 1967 (2nd edition).

Hitchcock, C. Leo and Arthur Cronquist. **Vascular Plants of the Pacific Northwest**. Seattle: University of Washington Press, 1972. (technical)

Hitchcock, C. Leo, Arthur Cronquist, Marion Ownbey, and J. W. Thompson. **Vascular Plants of the Pacific Northwest**. 5 vols. Seattle: University of Washington Press, 1955-1969. (technical)

Horn, Elizabeth. **Wildflowers 1 - The Cascades**. Touchstone Press, 1972.

Books with Both Plant Identifications and Recipes

Hall, Alan. **The Wild Food Trail Guide**. Holt, Rinehart and Winston, 1973.

Harrington, H. D. **Western Edible Wild Plants**. Albuquerque: The University of New Mexico Press, 1972.

Szczawinski, Adam F. and George A. Hardy. **Guide to Common Edible Plants of British Columbia**, British Columbia Provincial Museum, Department of Recreation and Conservation.

Books About Indian Usage of Plants

Gunther, Erna. **Ethnobotany of Western Washington**. Seattle: University of Washington Press, 1973

Murphey, Edith Van Allen. **Indian Uses of Native Plants**. Fort Bragg: Mendocino County Historical Society, 1959.

Books About Poisonous Plants

James, Wilma Roberts. **Know Your Poisonous Plants.** Healdsburg: Naturegraph Publishers, 1973.

Kingsbury, John M. **Deadly Harvest, A Guide to Common Poisonous Plants.** Holt, Rinehart and Winston, 1965.

Kingsbury, John M. **Poisonous Plants of the United States and Canada.** Englewood Cliffs: Prentice Hall Inc., 1964. (technical)

Muenscher, Walter Conrad. **Poisonous Plants of the United States.** New York: The Macmillan Company, 1951.

Wild Plants and Wild Animals

Martin, Alexander C., Herbert S. Zim, Arnold L. Nelson. **American Wildlife and Plants, A Guide to Wildlife Food Habits.** New York: Dover Publications, Inc., 1961.

Notes

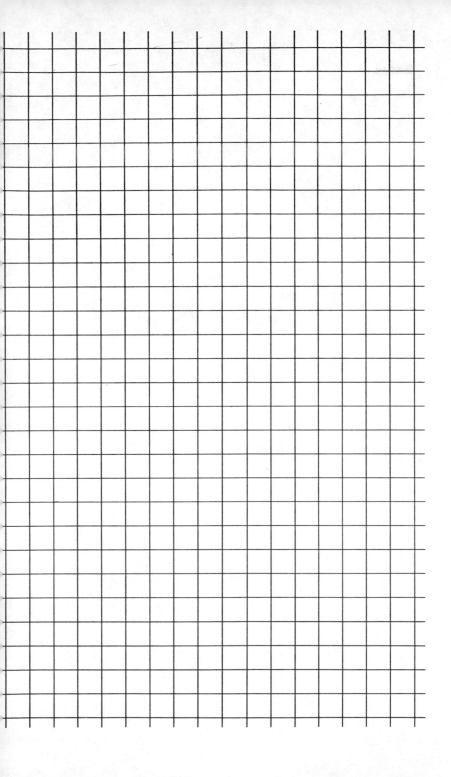

Notes

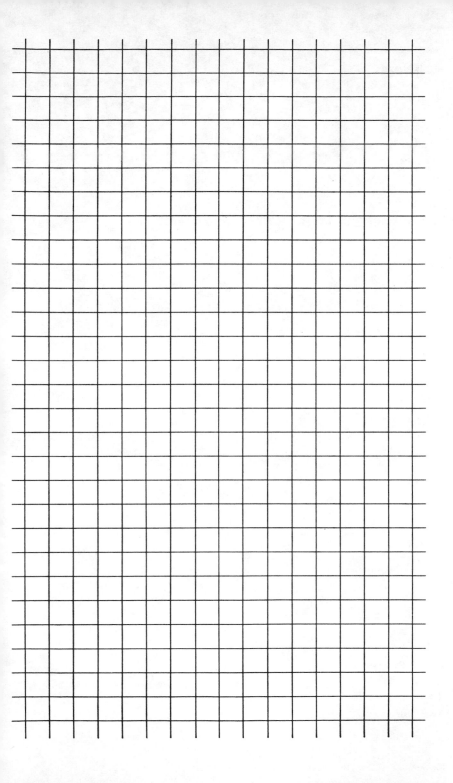

Notes

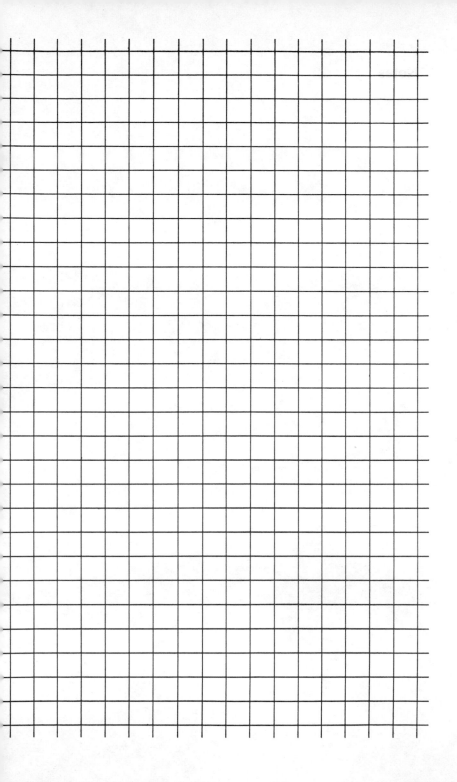

Notes

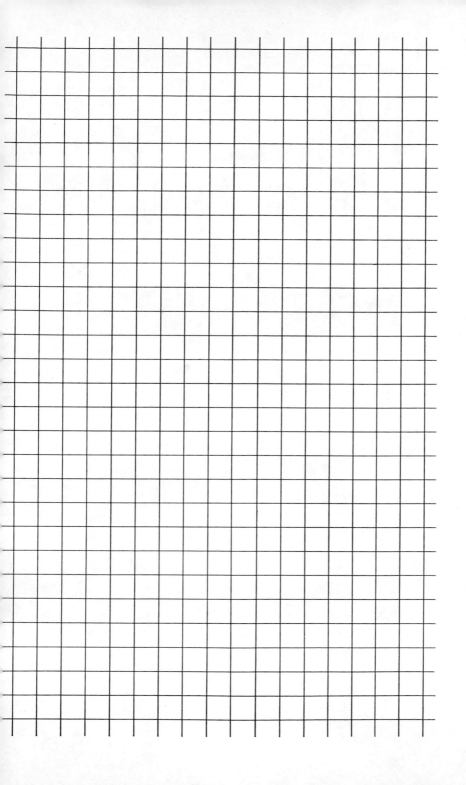

Notes

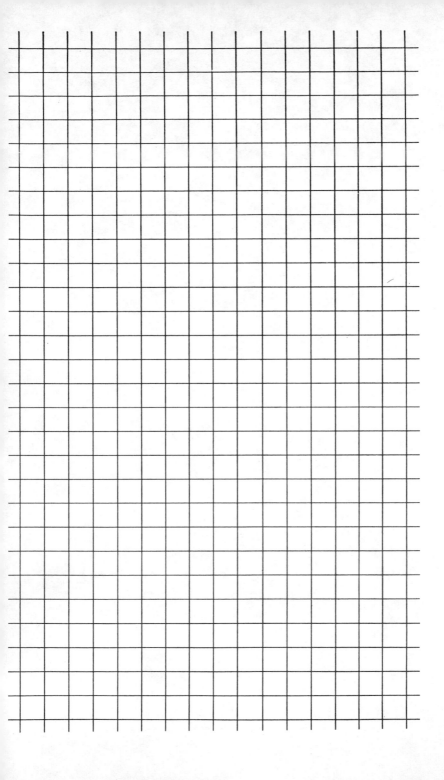